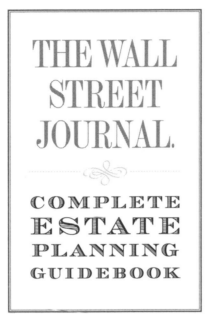

# THE WALL STREET JOURNAL.

## COMPLETE ESTATE PLANNING GUIDEBOOK

# THE WALL STREET JOURNAL.

## COMPLETE ESTATE PLANNING GUIDEBOOK

RACHEL EMMA SILVERMAN

CROWN
BUSINESS
NEW YORK

CROWN BUSINESS is a trademark and CROWN and the Rising Sun
colophon are registered trademarks of Random House, Inc.

Crown Business books are available at special discounts for bulk
purchases for sales promotions or corporate use. Special editions,
including personalized covers, excerpts of existing books, or books
with corporate logos, can be created in large quantities for special needs.
For more information, contact Premium Sales at (212) 572-2232 or
e-mail specialmarkets@randomhouse.com.

Library of Congress Cataloging-in-Publication Data

Silverman, Rachel Emma.
The Wall Street Journal complete estate-planning guidebook /
by Rachel Emma Silverman.—1st ed.
p. cm.
Includes bibliographical references and index.
1. Estate planning. 2. Finance, Personal. I. Wall Street Journal. II. Title.
HG179.S4746 2011
332.024'016—dc23          2011023496

ISBN 978-0-307-46127-8
eISBN 978-0-307-46128-5

Printed in the United States of America

Book design by Mauna Eichner and Lee Fukui
Cover illustration © Peter Hoey

10 9 8 7 6 5 4 3

First Edition

To Alex, Sam and Ethan,

for everything

# CONTENTS

# INTRODUCTION

You can't avoid death or taxes.

But by carefully drafting your will and medical directives, and by having clear discussions with your family, you can reduce the chances that your relatives will squabble over your medical care or your heirlooms. And while few people are subject to the federal estate tax under the recently passed tax law, if you're one of them, you can use strategies such as trusts, life insurance and philanthropy to vastly reduce the amount of money that goes to the tax man and increase what goes to your heirs or to the causes you believe in.

In *The Wall Street Journal Complete Estate-Planning Guidebook* I'll take you through the estate-planning process, step-by-step—from helping you figure out your planning goals (benefiting your children? minimizing estate taxes? caring for Fido?) to helping you divvy up your family's silver so your kids don't fight over it.

The book is structured around the main estate-planning tools you will likely encounter: wills, trusts, life insurance, guardianship papers, advance medical directives (which spell out your wishes in case you become severely incapacitated) and power-of-attorney documents (which grant another person the power to make decisions about your medical care or finances when you cannot). I'll also help you decode the technical jargon that estate planners often use, so you feel comfortable discussing QTIPs and QPRTs when you sit down with your lawyer.

Some situations require more complicated planning, so in special sections throughout the book, called "A Deeper Look," I'll talk about how to handle your estate if you're single, are in an unmarried or same-sex relationship, are in a remarriage or have a family member who is disabled or has special needs and you serve as a family caregiver. I'll also address the growing "asset protection" industry, which seeks to shield estates from the hands of creditors or divorcing spouses. And since many of us are pet owners, I'll discuss how to plan for our furry friends.

In the first chapter, "Getting Started," I'll cover key steps you should take before you and your lawyer draft your will, trust and other documents. Here, I will help you figure out your estate-planning goals, show you how to take stock of your possessions and provide strategies for talking these ideas over with your family. This chapter also offers guidance on how to choose a lawyer and other estate advisers. Clarifying your estate-planning objectives and discussing them with your family will likely save you money and time—and minimize arguments—in the long run. I'll also provide information here about key estate-planning steps to take at different stages in your life.

In Chapter Two, "Death and Taxes," I'll explain how estate, gift and generation-skipping taxes work and introduce some strategies to help minimize them. Under current law, these taxes affect just a small number of people, but it's still important to understand how they work.

In Chapter Three, "Wills," you'll learn why a will is the centerpiece of most estate plans and I'll go over some strategies to ensure that your money and belongings are left in the way that you choose. I'll discuss how to choose an executor and I'll explain the responsibilities of the role. I'll also go over when it may make sense to say no to an inheritance. I'll talk about how some estate plans may be equitable but not necessarily equal—and I'll offer some ideas about how to balance out bequests and gifts to heirs who may have very different economic and family circumstances.

While a will is an essential part of any estate plan, not all of your assets are governed by the terms of your will. In Chapter Four, "Probate and Ways to Avoid It," I'll explain how some key assets—including retirement plans, insurance policies, certain jointly owned property and some trusts—don't pass through wills and aren't subject to the legal process of probate. (Probate is a time-consuming court procedure that divides up your property as directed by your will.) I'll help you make sure your property goes to your intended heirs. I'll also talk about how to pass on individual retirement accounts, or IRAs, which are subject to all sorts of complex rules.

In Chapter Five, "Trusts," I'll discuss how trusts work. Contrary to popular belief, you don't need to be a Rockefeller to create a trust. In fact, many people without significant wealth use trusts for a variety of reasons, such as avoiding the hassles and expense of probate or providing for young children. You'll learn about the pros and cons of naming a family member or a financial services firm as your trustee and how to choose the right place to set up your trust. This chapter also includes a detailed Trust Tip Sheet, which decodes the alphabet soup of trust lingo that you may hear from your lawyer. I'll teach you how to structure trusts for minor children and spouses, how to create tax-saving trusts and how to pass on your house to heirs through a trust. In a special section in this chapter, "A Deeper Look," I'll show how to use trusts and other tactics to protect your assets from creditors and lawsuits.

In Chapter Six, "Life Insurance," I'll go over this valuable tool for providing for your family's future. I'll discuss the differences between term and permanent life insurance and how to best structure your life insurance policy to reduce estate taxes. And I'll go over some basic insurance, tax and estate-planning strategies for passing on family businesses.

In Chapter Seven, "Philanthropy," I'll discuss charitable

giving and how such generosity doesn't just help important causes but also can help you reduce taxes and provide for your family members. I'll talk about different ways to make charitable gifts, including direct bequests and charitable trusts, and I'll explain the pros and cons of setting up your own charitable foundation.

In Chapter Eight, "Preparing for the Unthinkable," I'll discuss other key estate-planning documents you'll need. These include papers naming a guardian for your children as well as powers of attorney for finances and health, crucial documents that name agents to make financial and medical decisions for you if you're unable to do so yourself. In a special section in this chapter, "A Deeper Look," I'll cover planning for family members with special needs. I'll also talk about making funeral and burial plans. And I'll address how to plan for your pets' care when you are not around.

In Chapter Nine, "Preserving Family Harmony," I'll go over some ways to help strengthen your estate plan to help prevent family feuds and challenges, especially when you're no longer able to voice your wishes. Here, I'll talk about feud defusers such as mediation, arbitration and no-contest clauses, which disinherit heirs if they protest your will. I'll address some estate-planning strategies for people who are in remarriages and may have both children and stepchildren. I'll give you ideas for dividing up personal property, such as jewelry and heirlooms, since tangible stuff with sentimental value often causes more rifts than cash does. In "A Deeper Look," I'll discuss an unusual but effective way to help keep family harmony: paying family members for their caregiving contributions if you or your spouse become incapacitated.

At this point you'll have learned how to draw up your will, trust and other estate documents. Congratulations! But you're not quite done yet. You still need to create a system for taking care of your estate plan over time. That's where Chapter Ten, "Maintaining Your Plan," comes in. I'll go over the "care and feeding" of your estate plan—how to store it and when to update it, and the importance of keeping your plans flexible.

In short, this book should provide you with the information you need to ensure that when you're gone, your hard-earned money goes where you want it to. That said, if your finances or family situation is unusually complex or your spouse or heirs are not U.S. citizens, I highly recommend also getting tailor-made legal and tax advice from qualified advisers who specialize in estate planning.

The more you plan ahead, the lower the chances of divisive family brawls and surprise tax bills. What's more, when you educate yourself about estate planning, you can reduce the number of expensive hours you spend with your lawyer and avoid sketchy tax shelters and other shams.

As you work through *The Wall Street Journal Complete Estate-Planning Guidebook,* rest assured that although you can't evade death or taxes, you can create an estate plan that will make both a whole lot easier for your loved ones. Your family will thank you for it.

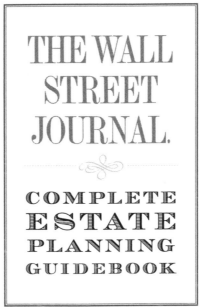

# THE WALL STREET JOURNAL.

## COMPLETE ESTATE PLANNING GUIDEBOOK

## CHAPTER 1

# GETTING STARTED

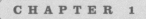

## WHY PLAN AHEAD?

Very few people want to think about their estate plan. Doing so means mulling over scary events in the future, such as death and incapacity, plus it can involve awkward conversations with family members.

But trust me, it's worth going through the psychological discomfort, time, expense and hassle of drawing up a will and other estate-planning documents. Why?

First off, writing a will and a detailed estate plan means that you're in control over how your property passes to your heirs or to charity when you're not around.

Without a will or other advance planning, your estate is what is called "intestate," which means that your property will be handled according to state law, rather than your wishes. Typically, if you die without an estate plan, your property will first go to your spouse, then to your children, then to their descendants, depending on your particular state's laws. (See www.mystatewill.com to find out what happens to your assets in your state if you die without a will.) Without an estate plan, you have little say over how much goes to whom and little control over which items go to loved ones or charities you may want to support.

## ESTATE-PLANNING ESSENTIALS

These are the key documents you should have in your estate plan, at a minimum. These should be up to date and reflect your current family and financial situation:

- **Will,** which outlines how your property is distributed to heirs

- **Power of attorney for finances,** naming someone to manage your financial affairs if you can't

- **Power of attorney for health care,** naming someone to manage health care decisions if you can't

- **Living will,** which outlines your end-of-life and disability preferences

- **Guardianship designation,** naming someone to raise your children if you pass away or become severely incapacitated

- **Completed beneficiary designation** forms for your retirement plans

What about a trust? As we'll discuss in Chapter Five, there are many different types of trusts, applicable to many different situations. For instance, a revocable living trust, intended for probate avoidance or property management, may be appropriate for you depending on where you live. Or another type of trust may be right if you expect to have a taxable estate or if you have young children. Trusts are fantastic tools, but they aren't always appropriate for everyone.

It's especially important to have a will if you want to leave assets to an unmarried partner, as I'll discuss further in "A Deeper Look," at the end of this chapter. Even if you've been together for years and live together, state law could dictate that your partner gets nothing, and he or she could even lose your shared home.

There are tax issues to consider as well. A small number of extremely wealthy families have estates that are subject to the federal estate tax, which can mean handing back more than a third of your cash to Uncle Sam at death. (I'll talk more about the estate tax in the next chapter.) If you're one of them, not to worry: there are a number of smart strategies, including using special trusts, life insurance and charitable donations, that can minimize this tax or eliminate it altogether and maximize what you are able to pass on to the people and causes that are important to you.

Planning your estate goes beyond just writing up a will or trust, however. It also means having arrangements in place so that someone can make medical and financial decisions on your behalf, in the way that you would like, if you are unable to do so someday. And it means naming someone to serve as a guardian for your children if you are unable to care for them.

The biggest mistake many people make is waiting too long before making all these kinds of decisions. Often families don't think about drafting medical instructions until a loved one is in the hospital and they face questions about medical care. Or a family may go through fractious court proceedings to name a guardian for an incapacitated parent because that parent failed to leave instructions in the case of severe disability.

It's far better to plan ahead. And it's never too early to start. Even if you're in your 20s or 30s, it's simply irresponsible not to have an estate plan, especially if you have children.

Believe me, planning your estate ahead of time will mean peace of mind for you and your loved ones. But before you get started, you need to figure out exactly what your estate-planning goals are.

## FIGURING OUT YOUR GOALS

Before heading down to the law office to have the attorneys write up a will, you need to figure out what your estate-planning goals are. Clarifying your main objectives ahead of time will save you time and money when you meet with your estate-planning advisers.

Among the many questions to consider:

- Do you want to leave money to family members?

- Are there other heirs you want to benefit?

- Do you want each child or heir to inherit equal amounts or do you want to vary the amounts depending on their family or economic situations?

- Do you have sufficient funds for your retirement?

- Do you want to make charitable bequests?

- Exactly what is the extent of your assets and your liabilities?

- Do you expect to have a taxable estate?

- Who would you want to be a guardian of your minor children?

- Who would you want to handle your financial affairs if you become incapacitated?

- Who would you want to handle your medical affairs if you become incapacitated?

- Who would you want to be the executor of your estate or the trustee of any trusts you set up?

- Do you want to leave specific objects or heirlooms to particular loved ones?

- Do you have specific wishes for your end-of-life care or if you become severely incapacitated?

- How should you best store and organize your estate-planning, financial and medical documents?

- How do your life insurance policies and retirement plans fit in with your estate plan?

- Are there other advisers you should consult?

- How can you best communicate your estate-planning wishes to your family?

Ask yourself what special concerns you may have:

- Do you or family members have any disabilities, chronic illnesses or other special needs?

- Are you remarried but have children from a previous relationship for whom you wish to provide?

- Are you in a contentious relationship with children or other family members?

- Do you want to disinherit anyone?

- Do you have pets you want to ensure are in good hands?

- Are you single or in an unmarried or same-sex relationship?

- Do you face decisions about how to pass on a family business?

- Are your spouse, children or parents not U.S. citizens?

- Do you or other family members have devout religious beliefs that may affect estate planning?

Write down the answers to each of these questions, as well as any special issues your estate plan needs to address, and bring this with you when you meet with your lawyer or estate planner. Many lawyers will also ask you to fill out forms before you meet with them, and the forms typically have questions to help you identify your estate-planning objectives, but again, the more planning you do in advance, the better.

## TALK IT OVER

Once you figure out your goals in creating an estate plan, it's important to keep your family and other loved ones in the know if you expect to name them as heirs or as guardians or agents who make decisions for you when you're unable to. The large-scale wealth that's been created in recent decades means more money is at stake for a lot of families—which can exacerbate preexisting tensions. Plus, divorces and remarriages can lead to conflicts among children and stepfamilies over inheritances. (I'll discuss planning for such blended families in Chapter Nine.)

Keeping your family informed early on can help to minimize family squabbles and to ensure that your wishes are carried out. This way, you can gauge your heirs' reactions to your estate plan and, if necessary, make changes to keep fighting at a minimum (or at the very least give your heirs time to work through any issues they may have with the plan).

You also want to make sure your estate plan coordinates with your parents' and adult children's own estate plans. For instance, if you might eventually be the beneficiary of a large inheritance from your parents, you need to consider that when devising your own plans. (See "Inheritor's Trusts" in Chapter Five for more information.)

No doubt it can be tough to talk about estate-planning issues with loved ones. Few people like to shine a light on their finances or discuss their inevitable death or decline. Some parents also worry that talking to their children about likely inheritances could cause heirs to become lazy or argumentative.

In some cases, it's because of generational differences, with younger families more willing to talk openly about family finances than their more tight-lipped ancestors. "Members of older generations were more reluctant to discuss these issues," said R. Hugh Magill, an executive at Northern Trust Corp. "The thought was, you don't talk about money."

On the other hand, many families find that their older relatives may actually be more than willing to talk about their estates or other uncomfortable topics such as end-of-life care or medical decision making, because those topics are top of mind for them. Holding such a conversation—addressing the proverbial elephant in the room—can sometimes come as a great relief.

All the same, bringing up estate planning can be an awkward conversation, even for the closest families. One lawyer I know suggested, only half jokingly, discussing it over a bottle of wine—or two. For many families, taking an indirect approach makes the topic easier to talk about. For instance, you might mention friends' experiences or prominent families in the news, such as the sordid estate contest involving the late *Playboy* playmate Anna Nicole Smith or the guardianship disputes after pop star Michael Jackson's death. Then segue into "Do you think we should talk about this stuff, too?"

You can also pass along estate-planning articles or books (such as this one) to family members and say, "I've been reading this book about responsible estate planning." Or you can mention your own estate-planning steps, such as the fact that you and your spouse just updated your own wills. "You might want to think about doing the same," you could say to relatives.

You can talk more generally about family goals and values—such as supporting a favorite cause, the importance of college education or a secure retirement, creating independent children and grandchildren—and ask how you can accomplish those wishes through an estate plan. It's also smart to accentuate the positive, by stressing how estate planning can benefit both parents and children and how the process is really an effort to honor family members' wishes. You can address how time-consuming and fractious things can be when families don't have well-organized, accessible estate plans. The more information everyone has, the easier it is to coordinate each family member's own estate plan.

You can also say that you want to make sure that you are aware of loved ones' wishes, for things such as medical care or the distribution of their possessions, so that these wishes are properly carried out when the time comes. Ask family members about any special requests they may have.

The website Who Gets Grandma's Yellow Pie Plate? (www .yellowpieplate.umn.edu), a project out of the University of Minnesota, has a terrific list of tips for talking about inheritance. Among the tips: ask what-if questions, such as "Dad, what would you want to have happen with the things in the house if you and Mom were no longer able to live here?"

Parents having these conversations with children may choose to address each child individually, asking what he or she expects and wants from the plan. That way, each child may feel freer to express his or her opinion—and parents can gather the information and figure out whether there are any potential conflicts.

Holding an organized family meeting, preferably in a relaxing place, such as a vacation home, is another way to get the process going. At these meetings, family members can ask questions and express opinions. Some families like to have a neutral third-party adviser, such as a lawyer or accountant, as a facilitator, to help defuse tensions that may arise while trying to hammer out tough issues, such as who gets what. Decide ahead of time whether you want to have just immediate family present for these meetings or include spouses of adult children.

Make sure everyone comes to the meeting prepared with a list of questions and concerns, such as how to access important financial, medical or estate-planning documents when the time comes and if family members have strong feelings they want to address about end-of-life care. Siblings can also meet ahead of time to come up with a list of questions and topics for a meeting with Mom and Dad.

However, I'd recommend that you avoid holding such discussions during times that can already be draining, such

## WHAT TO TALK ABOUT WHEN YOU TALK ABOUT ESTATE PLANNING

Here's a list of questions to bring up with your family when you discuss your plans:

- Do you feel comfortable about your financial situation? Do you have sufficient assets for your retirement? Would a financial or tax planner be helpful?

- Do you have a will? If so, where is it located?

- Who should handle your finances if you become unable to yourself? Have you granted someone a power of attorney for finances? If so, who has the power and where is the document located?

- Have you written a power of attorney for health care? If so, who has the power and where is the document located?

- Do you have a living will with end-of-life health care instructions? More specifically, if you become seriously ill, what level of care or intervention would you like?

- Do you have a safe-deposit box? Where is the box located and where is the key? Where is the list of contents?

- What is the location of essential personal papers—birth and marriage certificates, divorce papers, Social Security and military service records?

- Where are life, health and property insurance policies kept?

- Have you made a list of financial accounts and investments (savings accounts, certificates of deposit, stocks and bonds, credit cards) along with contact information for the institutions that hold the accounts?

- Have you made a list of the personal and real property that you own? Where is the list located?

- Are there any assets, such as artwork, heirlooms or a house, that you have specific wishes for?

- Who are your legal, tax and financial advisers and where is their contact information?

- Do you have any instructions for your funeral or disposition of your remains?

- Do you have organ donation wishes?

- If you have a retirement plan, is there a death benefit for survivors? If so, what is the contact information?

- If you have a family business, have you taken steps to plan for its future when you are gone?

- Do you wish to make any philanthropic bequests?

- Have you made any plans for the care of your pets?

*Source: Adapted from Marsha A. Goetting, extension family economics specialist and professor, Montana State University, Bozeman, and Vicki L. Schmall, Ph.D., former extension gerontology specialist and professor, Oregon State University, Corvallis; Oast & Hook, P.C.*

as soon after a loved one's death or even during holiday get-togethers (if such gatherings are particularly stressful in your family). And if an organized meeting is too tough, you may want to try a relaxing activity, such as walking or golfing, which can help reduce tensions during stressful conversations.

Bear in mind that despite your best attempts at conversation, some family members may still be reluctant to join the discussion or communicate their feelings. Keeping silent, though, can ultimately be a recipe for disaster. "Most fights and problems are simply because of not being up-front about things," said Paramus, New Jersey, estate lawyer Martin Shenkman. "You need to be on the straight and narrow, because when you start to arouse suspicions it just gets worse."

What's more, listening to other family members share their wishes can help you clarify your own estate-planning goals or bring up issues or questions that you may not have thought of before.

## CHOOSING ADVISERS

Picking the right lawyer is the next step in preparing your estate. Estate and trust law varies dramatically by state, so it's best to find a lawyer in your area who is familiar with applicable state laws. Because there are many smart tax-saving strategies or potential legal pitfalls that a non-expert may not be familiar with, it's also smart to use a lawyer who specializes in trusts and estates, rather than a more general lawyer, especially if you have a large estate or a complicated family situation.

Most people find their lawyers through word of mouth, so it's a good idea to ask your friends and family members for referrals. (One caveat: if you use the same lawyer as another family member, such as your parents, make sure that the lawyer is truly representing you, if your interests and those of your parents differ.)

Another resource for finding good estate lawyers is the American College of Trust and Estate Counsel, or ACTEC (www.actec.org), a professional organization of top estate lawyers. The site has a searchable database to help you find qualified counsel in your area. You can also go to the American Bar Association website (www.findlegalhelp.org) or contact your local bar association to find a specialized estate lawyer near you.

If you are a senior citizen or want to help an elderly family member, you may want to consult an attorney who specializes in elder law. Such a lawyer can be especially helpful when trying to figure out the intricacies of government benefits, such as Medicare or Medicaid, or in planning for the possibility of nursing home care or the possibility of incapacity. See the National Academy of Elder Law Attorneys (www.naela.org) to find an elder law attorney near you.

Once you get a few names, you'll want to call each of the

## WHAT ABOUT DO-IT-YOURSELF WILLS?

Estate-planning software and websites can be money savers, especially if you have a simple estate plan with no estate tax issues. If you're leaving the bulk of your estate to your spouse or kids, this may be an alternative worth considering.

There are a range of products, such as Quicken WillMaker Plus, which is updated each year and downloadable at www.nolo.com. The program can help you create a range of documents, including living trusts or health care directives. Other popular estate-planning programs can be found at www.buildawill.com and www.legalzoom.com.

Estate-planning experts agree that any will, even it a do-it-yourself one aided by websites, software or books, is typically better than none at all, especially if you have a straightforward financial and family situation. But make sure that a do-it-yourself plan takes into account state laws, which vary. For instances, each state has a different requirement for how your will signing must be witnessed.

However, if you have complex estate issues, such as a large, taxable estate, real estate in different states, a special-needs child or a fractious family situation, consult a lawyer. Yes, it's more expensive—typically starting at about $1,500 to put together basic estate-planning documents, compared to prices starting at under $100 for online forms. But a lawyer can help you come up with strategies and plans tailor-made to your particular situation and to your state's laws, as well as testify to your competence if the plan is ever challenged, and may very well end up saving you and your heirs money in the long run.

lawyers to set up a consultation. During this initial phone call, be sure to ask about their process and fee structure. Most lawyers charge by the hour; rates vary dramatically by location and also by the experience of the lawyer. Other attorneys, meanwhile, charge a flat fee—typically several thousand dollars—for a suite of estate-planning documents, including a will and health care directives.

## INTERVIEWING A LAWYER

Here are some questions to consider when vetting potential lawyers. Shopping around is worth it, both financially and for peace of mind:

- Ask about fee structure. Do they charge by the hour or a flat rate?

- Are follow-up phone calls, emails and photocopies free or not?

- Does the lawyer specialize in estate planning?

- Is the firm large or a small boutique?

- Explain succinctly your family's situation and ask what sort of planning they'd recommend—and a ballpark estimate for the documents.

- Does the firm have other clients in your financial or family situation—or would you be an outlier?

- Does the lawyer seem to have values that you agree with?

- Do you have a rapport with the lawyer on the phone—does he or she seem to "get" you?

Be careful, though. Some lawyers charge for every email, phone call and photocopy. (I've experienced this personally, when I received large bills for what I thought were routine email responses from my lawyer.) Also ask whether follow-up phone calls or emails are free or not. I'm not recommending that you necessarily go with a bargain-basement lawyer; you simply want to make sure that you are getting more value if one lawyer is charging you substantially more than another.

Ask about the firm's size—is it a large firm with deep expertise or a small boutique with fewer clients but very personal service? Do the lawyers or their firms solely focus on estate planning or do they practice in many areas of the law?

Explain to each lawyer you meet with, as succinctly as possible, your family's situation, and then ask what sort of planning he or she would recommend and a ballpark estimate for the documents. Does the firm have other clients in your

## AN ESTATE-PLANNING TEAM

Your estate-planning team might include other professionals in addition to your lawyer. You might need to hire an accountant or financial planner to help you with estate tax planning or business planning. The American Institute of Certified Public Accountants (www.aicpa.org), can help you find a qualified accountant in your area.

The Financial Planning Association (www.fpanet.org) lists Certified Financial Planners who can help you with investments or general financial planning. Alternatively, you may want to consider a fee-only financial planner. These advisers don't get paid commissions for recommending financial services products, so they may make less compromised recommendations. You can find a fee-only planner at the National Association of Personal Financial Advisors (www.napfa.org).

If your estate plan involves life insurance, you might need to contact an insurance broker or agent to help you secure the right policy for you. The National Association of Insurance and Financial Advisors (http://www.naifa .org) can help you locate an insurance professional.

Finally, you may need an appraiser to help you determine the value of your property or business interests. Appraisers can be found through the website of the American Society of Appraisers, www.appraisers.org.

financial or family situation, or would you be an outlier? Does the lawyer seem to have values that you agree with? (Some lawyers, for instance, focus on Christian estate planning or gay and lesbian estate planning.)

Above all, do you have a rapport with the lawyer on the phone? In other words, does he or she seem to "get" you? This isn't a trivial issue. After all, he or she will know everything about your finances, and perhaps your family's dirty laundry, so you really want someone you can trust and with whom you can have a close long-term relationship with and open lines of communication.

On that note, it's crucial that you be 100% honest about your financial, family and health conditions when you meet with your estate-planning lawyer. That can sometimes be painful, especially if you are dealing with a fractured family, a child's drug abuse, an out-of-wedlock child or a business on the brink of failure. What's more, since a number of estate-planning tools are based on potential life expectancy, it's important to be up-front about any health problems you or your spouse are facing.

My husband and I interviewed three lawyers over the phone before we finally settled on one. We liked his phone manner and his fee schedule—he charged a flat fee for estate-planning documents, rather than billing by the hour. Our initial face-to-face meeting with him, which lasted an hour and a half, went very well and we liked the plan he suggested for us.

However, after our initial meeting he wasn't responsive to our phone calls and questions. It turned out he was simply overwhelmed by other clients. After a month or so of unreturned phone calls, we switched to another lawyer, who ended up working out for us.

The lesson: you might not find the right match on your first try, so it pays to talk to several lawyers and hold out on a decision until you find one you're comfortable with.

## TAKING STOCK

So you've chosen a lawyer, based on phone consultations, experience, word of mouth and fees. He or she will typically ask you to fill out a questionnaire before an initial face-to-face meeting. (If your lawyer has a website, you may be able to download the questionnaires.)

Typically, these forms ask you to take stock of what you own in order to determine what's in your estate. You'll list your employment and investment income; assets, including bank accounts, investment accounts, CDs, retirement plans, insurance policies, annuities, vehicles and business interests; real estate; liabilities, including mortgages, car loans and outstanding credit card debt; and any special art, jewelry, furniture and collectibles. You should also list any intangible property, such as patents or other intellectual property. Also note any possible windfalls or inheritances you expect to receive down the road.

Next, you'll need to note how the property is titled—is it in your name, in a spouse's name or owned jointly with your spouse or another person? It's key to determine ownership so that the appropriate owners can have control over how their assets are handled. In a nutshell, assets owned by you are considered part of your estate. If they are owned by another person, such as your spouse, or by another entity, such as an irrevocable trust or partnership, they're generally out of your estate and not counted for estate tax purposes. Once such assets are out of your estate, you have no direct control over them. Meanwhile, if you own property jointly with another person, the rules are more complex and can vary by state law, so I'll go into more detail about joint property in Chapters Three and Four.

The purpose of inventorying your assets is twofold: to take stock of your possessions so you can determine how you want to leave them, and also to see if your estate is large enough to be subject to estate taxes, which can mean taking extra measures to minimize the tax.

Then the questionnaire will usually get down to the nitty-gritty of how you want to leave your property and how you want the rest of your affairs handled, including any special instructions. For instance, your lawyer may ask if you have any charitable bequests or if you have any pets that need to be cared for.

The questionnaire might also ask you to name specific people to handle certain tasks. For instance, the worksheet may require you to name an executor, the person who handles the distribution of your estate after you are deceased. (You'll also be asked to name a successor executor, in case the person or institution you named isn't up to the task.) You will likely

## INVENTORYING YOUR ASSETS AND LIABILITIES

Before drawing up your estate plan, you need to gather a complete list of your assets and liabilities—and determine whether they are owned solely by you or jointly with your spouse or another person.

**Assets**

- Bank accounts, including savings and checking accounts
- Investment accounts and securities, including mutual funds, stocks and bonds
- CDs
- Cash
- Retirement plans, including IRAs and 401(k)s
- Insurance policies
- Annuities
- Vehicles or boats
- Real estate and property
- Artwork, jewelry, furniture, collectibles or other personal valuables that are important to your family
- Business interests, including partnerships or corporations
- Patents, royalties or other intellectual property
- Outstanding loans owed to you, such as personal loans

**Liabilities**

- Mortgages
- Auto loans
- Outstanding credit card debt
- Outstanding bank loans
- Outstanding taxes or liens

## ESTATE PLANNING THROUGHOUT YOUR LIFETIME

Estate planning isn't just for senior citizens. It's important to have key documents, such as a will, an advance medical directive and power-of-attorney documents, no matter how old you are. Here are some estate key estate-planning steps to take at different stages of your life:

- **Anyone over 18.** Since incapacity can strike at any time, all adults should have a power of attorney for finances and health care and an advance medical directive specifying your wishes if you become critically ill. Also make sure to fill out beneficiary designation forms on your retirement accounts, since these assets pass directly to heirs without a will.

- **You are young and single.** In addition to the documents named above, you should write a will so that any wealth or material possessions you leave behind will go to whomever you choose (such as your parents, your significant other, siblings, relatives, friends or charity).

- **You are part of an unmarried couple.** If you are committed to a partner but not legally married, you need a will if you want your property to pass to your partner at your death. (Without a will, your partner may get nothing.) If you share valuable property, such as a house, consider owning the property as "joint tenants with rights of survivorship," which means that if one of you dies, the jointly held property will automatically pass to the surviving partner.

- **You are part of a married couple.** Because you are legally married, your estate can pass to your spouse free of estate taxes. (However, the surviving spouse may still have a taxable estate.) Also consider buying life insurance so that your spouse is provided for financially.

- **You are married with children.** You and your spouse should each have your own will, naming guardians for your minor children, in case both of you die simultaneously. (If you fail to name a guardian, a court will name someone, who may not be the person you would prefer.) You may want to create a trust to manage your children's assets in case you and your spouse pass away when they are minors. You should also buy life insurance to provide for your family.

- **You have accumulated significant wealth.** If you are worried you may have a taxable estate, talk to an estate-planning lawyer who can advise you on smart tax strategies, such as making annual gifts to family members or directly paying relatives' tuition or medical expenses, to reduce the size of your estate. (Estate tax planning is not an area where you want to wing it on your own.)

- **You are a senior citizen or are ill.** Make sure to update your will, powers of attorney and health care directives. Also consider a revocable living trust, naming a trustee who can manage your assets if you are unable to. Talk to your family about your wishes and make sure they have copies of your important estate-planning and financial documents.

*Source: Adapted from the California Society of CPAs (www.calcpa.org)*

also need to name a guardian, who can care for any minor children, typically those under age eighteen.

The questionnaire will provide the basis for the documents that your lawyer will eventually draw up for you. The purpose is to make you think through these important decisions ahead of time so you don't waste hours and dollars doing it while sitting in your lawyer's office.

## A DEEPER LOOK
# ESTATE PLANNING IF YOU'RE UNMARRIED

These days, fewer people are living in traditional Ozzie and Harriet–style relationships, with a husband, wife and a couple of kids. There are domestic partnerships, gay marriages and unmarried individuals who have rich relationships with families, partners or friends for whom they want to provide.

There has been a huge increase in cohabitating couples in recent decades. As of 2008, there were some 6.2 million unmarried-partner households in the United States, a category that encompasses both straight and gay couples, according to census data.

It's not just young people testing the waters before marriage. Many seniors choose not to marry because they don't want to complicate their inheritance plans or lose access to their pensions or health insurance.

One couple I interviewed, a widow and a widower in their late 70s, lived together for several years but decided not to marry because the widow would lose the pension from her late husband. "My income would be cut by five hundred dollars a month if I got married, and we can't afford that," she said.

Despite the big changes in recent years, unmarried couples remain second-class citizens in some key areas such as inheritance, retirement benefits and health care. For instance, husbands and wives can pass unlimited amounts of money to each other free of estate taxes, but unmarried couples cannot. And if one spouse dies, the other can automatically receive his or her Social Security benefits, while unmarried couples can't pass on benefits. Married couples may also be able to make medical decisions for their spouses without powers of attorney, but unmarried couples may have more trouble doing so. In good news for unmarried couples, though, President Obama recently ordered most hospitals to allow patients to designate whom they want to have visitation rights. (In the past, many hospitals only allowed family members related by blood or marriage to visit patients in critical care.)

For same-sex couples, filing tax returns and other personal finance documents can get very complicated, because of the patchwork quilt of same-sex marriage, civil union and domestic partnership laws in a handful of states. Because the federal government doesn't recognize same-sex relationships for tax purposes, gay couples must file their federal tax returns as single people, even if they can file as married in their home states.

Despite these hurdles, many unmarried couples are taking matters into their own hands to provide for their loved ones or better protect their assets, especially in the case of a death or breakup.

Attorneys recommend that single people or unmarried couples take several key planning steps:

**Write a will.** If a married person dies without a will, assets usually go tax-free to the surviving spouse. However, with unmarried couples, the lack of a will means that surviving family members—no matter how estranged—could claim the assets. The best way to protect against this is to write an ironclad will that specifically bequeaths assets to the unmarried partner.

If you're unmarried or in a same-sex marriage and have a very large estate, you can't pass money directly to your partner free of estate tax. (Only married husbands and wives can do this.) But you can help reduce the size of your estate by making annual gifts to benefit your partner.

**Change beneficiary designations.** Retirement plans, financial accounts and life insurance policies need current beneficiary designations to provide for your loved ones.

Recent legislation allowed non-spouse beneficiaries of retirement plans to take over their partner's 401(k) plan without a big tax penalty. (Before the legislation, only married spouses could inherit a 401(k) without an immediate tax hit.)

It's smart to take out life insurance policies on each other, especially if you and your partner share house payments or have kids.

Also, make sure your home, stock and investment accounts are properly titled, either jointly, in your name or in your partner's name, to reflect how you want the property to be owned and transferred.

**Plan ahead for housing.** Determining ownership—and doing some advance planning—can be especially important when it comes to housing. If you solely own the home that you and your partner live in together, your partner possibly could be booted out after you die unless you make proper arrangements, such as a life estate, letting your partner stay there. (I'll discuss life estates in Chapter Nine.)

**Draft a durable power of attorney for health care and finances.** These are documents authorizing your partner to make decisions for you if you become unable to take care of yourself. (See Chapter Eight for more information.)

**Create a parenting agreement.** If you and your partner have, or plan to have, children, you should consult with a family law attorney to come up with a plan, such as a joint custody or adoption agreement, that's appropriate for your family's situation. If you want your partner to be your child's guardian, be sure to make it official, to prevent any custody battles down the road.

**Create a cohabitation agreement.** These are like prenuptial agreements without the nuptials. These contracts, also called "living-together agreements," parse out how the furniture, car, house, bills and even pets should be divvied up during, and after, the relationship. While these are more applicable in the case of a breakup as opposed to a death, they are still a smart way for unmarried couples to protect their financial interests, because laws are murky and varied when an unmarried couple breaks up.

You might want to consider drafting one if you expect to stay together, without getting married, for the foreseeable future or if you are raising a child together. You should also create a contract if you and your partner are buying a big piece of property together, such as a house or car, or if one or both parties have significant assets. Other reasons to create a cohabitation agreement: one partner moves across the country, leaves a job or changes life in a drastic way for the relationship, or there's a large income disparity or one partner supports the other financially.

In some cohabitation agreements, couples agree to provide support payments in the case of a breakup; some couples choose to keep their finances completely separate. If you are both broke, such contracts can still be helpful to outline how expenses and debt should be divided.

If you buy a house together, you should also create a property agreement specifying what percentage each partner owns, how much each contributed to the down payment and mortgage and how the house should be divided if you break up.

One Cambridge, Massachusetts, couple I interviewed had a house management agreement that stipulated steps to take if the pair broke up. Among the contract's provisions: they would try couples therapy for six months if their relationship went on the rocks, and they wouldn't change the locks on the house.

For same-sex couples seeking more information on estate and financial planning, see www.prideplanners.com, www .outestateplanning.com and www.rainbowlaw.com.

## CHAPTER 2

# DEATH AND TAXES

Estate planning is ultimately about how to pass on your money, property and values to the people and causes you love. But for a very small group of wealthy people, estate planning takes on an added dimension: how to navigate taxes that are levied when you transfer property from one person to another.

Among these transfer taxes are federal and state estate taxes, which are imposed on the estates of only the very richest people when they die; gift taxes, which are owed if you make very large transfers of assets to other people while you're still alive; and generation-skipping transfer taxes, which are levied if you transfer very big sums of money to grandchildren or great-grandchildren. This chapter will explain how these taxes work and offer some strategies to help minimize them. (More transfer tax savings techniques are in Chapters Five, Six and Seven.)

Note that when I refer to the "estate tax" in the book, I am referring to the federal estate tax, unless otherwise specified.

## CONTROVERSY AND COMPLEXITY

The estate tax is both controversial and complex. Critics of the tax, who often call it a "death tax," argue that families who have built wealth should be able to distribute as much of it to their heirs as they like, without having Uncle Sam take back nearly half. They also argue that some of the money, such as income, may have already been taxed.

Proponents, meanwhile, say that the estate tax can prevent the formation of family dynasties, help redistribute wealth to the less fortunate, fund important public services and government programs and benefit charities.

The estate tax is complex because the rules governing it change frequently. Indeed, in the past three years, four different estate tax rules have been in effect. In 2008 the amount that individuals could shelter from the tax was $2 million; in 2009 it was $3.5 million; in 2010 the estate tax lapsed altogether, so there was an unlimited exemption; and in 2011 the exemption is $5 million (indexed for inflation in 2012). Whether the current tax rules continue for 2013 and beyond depends on the whims of Congress and the country's finances at the time.

It's important to note that under current tax rules, the vast majority of estates are exempt from the federal estate tax, which means they pay no estate taxes at all. Only about 3,600 estates will be subject to the federal estate tax under the $5 million exemption, estimates the nonpartisan Tax Policy Center. That's just 0.001% of the U.S. population.

But be aware that the latest estate tax rules are only temporary and slated to change yet again in 2013, unless Congress votes to extend current law. What happens to estate plans made now if the exemption for estate and gift taxes is lowered? There's a chance that future laws could be retroactive, which means that current moves may be invalidated. But estate planners say not to plan for that unlikely event. Instead, make plans under current law, keep them flexible and adjust as laws (and your own family's finances) change. For instance, include provisions in your will and trusts that give beneficiaries or trustees the power to make changes depending on the laws and family financial situations at the time of death, rather than making the estate plan too rigid.

"The reality is even if they finally come to an agreement

about the estate tax, for most of our clients the laws will change many, many more times before they die," said Las Vegas estate lawyer Steven Oshins. "It would be shortsighted to react too strongly to what is taking place in the near future and fail to see the big picture. If the person is wealthy, somehow the IRS is going to tax them, regardless of what particular year that person ends up dying."

Throughout the book, I'll address numerous other tax-saving strategies, such as the use of various trusts and philanthropic vehicles. The challenge, of course, is to have plans that are flexible enough to still be applicable as laws and circumstances change.

# THE ESTATE TAX: HOW IT WORKS

The estate tax is levied on the value of the assets—typically, your house, financial accounts, retirement plans and personal property, such as your art and jewelry—that you leave behind when you die.

The government allows you to shelter a certain amount of money from estate taxes, which is called the "estate tax exemption." There are also exemptions for gift and generation-skipping taxes. In 2011 the estate, gift and generation-skipping

| TRANSFER TAX RATES AND EXEMPTIONS | |
|---|---|
| Year: | 2011 |
| Estate and lifetime gift tax exemption (per individual): | $5 million (indexed for inflation in 2012) |
| Portable? | Yes |
| Tax rate: | 35% |
| Generation-skipping tax exemption (per individual): | $5 million (indexed for inflation in 2012) |
| Portable? | No |
| Tax Rate: | 35% |

tax exemptions are all $5 million for individuals (or $10 million for married couples) and the remainder is taxed at 35%. In 2012 that $5 million exemption will be indexed for inflation, so it may rise even higher. Taken together, these new estate, gift and generation-skipping tax rates are some of the most generous in decades, tax historians say.

Remember, though, that the latest estate tax rules are slated to change yet again in 2013, unless Congress votes to extend current law.

Married couples have a special advantage over single people or unmarried partners when it comes to estate taxes. A husband and wife can leave an unlimited amount of money and property to each other without it being subject to the estate tax—but taxes ultimately may be owed when the surviving spouse dies, if the estate is large enough. (Exceptions to the tax-free transfer between spouses are if one spouse is not a U.S. citizen, which I'll talk about further below, and same-sex spouses, whose marital status is not recognized by the federal government.) Money left to charities also doesn't count toward the tax.

In the previous chapter, I talked about how you can calculate your estate's worth. You tally up a list of all of your assets to calculate the gross value, and then subtract any debts, funeral or burial expenses, administrative costs paid to executors and trustees, as well as money bequeathed to charity or left for a spouse, to get the net value of your estate.

The value of your estate for estate tax purposes is typically assessed on the date of death. However, some executors and heirs choose to use what's called the "alternate valuation date," which is six months after the date of death. (The alternate valuation date may be useful during an economic downturn, which can depress the value of an estate, making it worth less for tax purposes.)

If your estate has a gross value greater than the federal exemption at the time of death, then your executor must file a federal estate tax return, IRS Form 706, available at the Internal Revenue Service website, www.irs.gov. (Note that your executor will still need to file an estate tax return even if your *net* estate—after liabilities, funeral and administrative expenses, and bequests to a spouse and charitable gifts—is less than the exemption amount.)

Estate tax returns are due within nine months after a death, although your executor can ask the IRS for a six-month extension.

## PORTABILITY

A notable feature of the recent estate tax changes is that the exemption is "portable." That means that each partner of a married couple can use the rest of the other's unused estate tax exemption. After the death of the first spouse, any unused portion of the spouse's $5 million exemption may go to the surviving partner's future estate. (Same-sex married couples, however, cannot take advantage of portability, because their marital status is not recognized by the federal government.)

Let's say I've made $2 million in lifetime gifts to my kids but left everything else outright to my husband. Because the estate and gift tax rules are tied in what's called a "unified credit," that $2 million is subtracted from my $5 million estate tax exemption upon my death. Here's where portability kicks in: after my death, the remaining $3 million left in my exemption carries over to my husband (as long as my executor remembers to file an estate tax return), who can shield $8 million of assets from estate taxes.

In the past, each partner of a married couple had always been allowed a full individual estate tax exemption. But married couples who left the bulk of their assets to their spouses often lost the value of one of their exemptions unless they set up special trusts, called "bypass" or "credit shelter" trusts. While such trusts are still valuable (I'll discuss them more in Chapter Five), portability makes them less necessary for some

## STEPPING UP

A very important tax issue to bear in mind is what's known as the "step-up" in cost basis. This is the system for valuing stocks, mutual fund shares and other inherited property whose value has increased over the years.

The step-up system is important to your heirs, because it can affect how much they might owe in capital gains taxes when they sell the property they inherit.

Here's how the step-up system generally works. Suppose in your will you leave your son stock you bought for $10,000 many years ago. On the day you die, the stock is now worth $200,000. At that point your son's "cost basis"— the value of the shares for income tax purposes—would be stepped up to $200,000, rather than the original purchase price of $10,000. That means your son would likely pay very little in capital gains taxes if he sold those shares soon after inheriting them. That's because capital gains taxes are fig- ured by subtracting the cost basis—now $200,000—from the current market value at which he sells the stocks.

However, gifts made during your lifetime don't receive a step-up in basis, unlike assets left in your estate. So if you give your son those shares during your lifetime, your original $10,000 cost basis carries over to him. That means that if your son sells those shares, he might owe hefty capital gains taxes. But if the stock was bequeathed to him in your estate, its cost basis would rise to full market value at death.

Note that for 2010, the year that the estate tax disappeared, the laws re- garding step-up in basis changed as well. If a loved one died in 2010, seek a lawyer for advice about your situation.

couples. Portability also makes planning easier when one spouse has a large, indivisible asset, such as an IRA, which can have only one owner at a time.

What happens to portability if one spouse remarries? In what some observers are calling a "black widow" provision, the new estate tax laws prohibit individuals from accumulating multiple $5 million exemptions through remarriages. You can use only the remaining exemption of your most recent spouse.

Note that in order for portability to be in effect, after you die your executor must actually transfer your unused exemption to your surviving spouse. Your executor must file an estate tax return within nine months of your death (or fifteen months with an extension), even if you don't owe any tax. If your executor fails to file the return, your surviving spouse can't use your unused exemption.

## STATE ESTATE TAXES

Adding to the confusion, more states have begun imposing their own estate taxes to raise revenues. Nearly half of the states now levy some form of tax at death, so you may end up owing both state and federal estate taxes. A few states also have inheritance taxes, which are imposed on beneficiaries who inherit property; tax rates and exemptions vary depending on the relationship of the beneficiary to the deceased.

State legislatures are regularly fiddling with their estate taxes, so laws change frequently. To find out more about whether your state has an estate or inheritance tax, or to find state estate tax forms, contact your estate lawyer and your state's department of revenue.

Making things tricky is that some states have much lower estate tax exemptions than the federal exemption. That means that more money may be subject to estate taxes in your state than under federal rules (although state tax *rates,* if you are over the exemption, are lower than the federal tax rate). New Jersey's estate tax exemption in 2011, for instance, was only $675,000, but the tax rate was 16%. So estates of New Jersey residents (as well as those who own real estate in New Jersey) are likely to owe the tax if they are worth more than $675,000, even though that's well under the current 2011 federal exemption of $5 million.

So what can you do if you live in a state, such as New Jersey, with an estate tax? For one thing, as I stress throughout this chapter and the book, create a flexible estate plan that allows you to make changes as state and federal laws change.

Under today's generous gift tax rules, giving your heirs money during your lifetime, rather than leaving them a bundle at death, can also help you save on state estate taxes. The tactic will help reduce the size of your estate to state and federal taxing authorities. (Most states don't impose state gift taxes, but check if that's the case in your state.)

A more drastic approach: move. Indeed, some estate lawyers are urging wealthy clients in high-tax areas, such as New York and New Jersey, to consider moving to places with no state estate tax, such as Florida. (But make sure to make the move official by registering to vote, getting a driver's license, registering your car, executing a will and changing your address on bills and other important documents in your new state.)

A handful of states let married couples put the amount of money subject only to state estate tax into a special trust called a "state qualified terminable interest property trust," or state QTIP trust. (I'll go over QTIPs in more detail in Chapter Five.) These trusts provide a surviving spouse with an income stream but delay estate tax until after the surviving spouse dies. Check with your lawyer to see if this is an option in your state.

Things can get complicated for those who live in a state with no estate tax but have second homes in taxable states. One idea that may work, depending on state law: place the taxable state's property into an entity such as a limited liability company (LLC). When property is in an LLC, it may be taxed under the estate tax laws of the state you live in, rather than those of the state where the property is located.

## THE GIFT TAX

The estate and generation-skipping taxes aren't the only ones that estate planners need to worry about. There's also the gift tax to bear in mind. The gift tax works as a stopgap to the estate tax: it prevents very wealthy people from giving all their money to their children before they die in order to avoid the estate tax.

The federal gift tax is only levied when you make gifts in your lifetime totaling more than $5 million (the exemption in 2011 and indexed for inflation in 2012) to anyone else. That exemption is a big jump from the $1 million gift tax exemption in recent years. Under the new law, the federal gift tax rate is 35%. (Note that currently Connecticut and Tennessee also levy state gift taxes, so make sure to check with a lawyer where you live, as laws change.)

Also note that spouses can give unlimited amounts to each other tax-free. Exceptions are if one spouse is not a U.S. citizen, which we'll discuss further below, and same-sex spouses, whose marital status is not recognized by the federal government.

Under the complicated laws governing the gift tax, there's also what's called an annual gift tax exclusion. In 2011, you can give away as much as $13,000 each to anyone you want—and to as many people as you wish—without any gift tax considerations or without reporting the gift to the IRS. In other words, you can give up to $13,000 to an unlimited number of people or to a trust—to your kids, to your nieces and nephews, to friends in need, to a trust to benefit your children—as long as you make each gift to a different individual or trust. The gift tax exclusion is indexed for inflation and typically rises every few years. Also, your gift may be cash or a non-cash item, such as stock or jewelry.

Married couples can give up to $26,000 this year, and if they make a special election on their gift tax return, the entire $26,000 can come from one partner's assets or from a joint account.

So if you and your spouse have three children, together you could give them a total of $78,000 per year, without this counting as a taxable gift. (In other words, you could give each of your three children $13,000 and your spouse could give each child $13,000, totaling $78,000.) But if you make gifts over the annual exclusion—say, $14,000 per child in 2011—the extra amount counts toward your $5 million lifetime total. For instance, if I gave my son $50,000 this year, $37,000 ($50,000 minus $13,000) would be counted against the lifetime exemption of $5 million.

How does the IRS track this? If you give away money over the amount of the gift tax exclusion, you need to file a gift tax return. (That's IRS Form 709, available at www.irs.gov; you file gift tax returns alongside your regular income tax returns.) But no gift tax is actually *due* until you have given away more than $5 million in taxable gifts (the current lifetime exemption).

Note that any taxable gifts during your lifetime will reduce, dollar for dollar, the amount you can shelter from the estate tax when you die. So let's say you're single and made a $3 million taxable gift during your lifetime. That means your estate can leave only $2 million to heirs free of estate tax.

Unlike charitable gifts, you can't deduct gifts to other people on your income tax forms. But on the plus side, *recipients* of gifts do not owe income taxes on the money; in most cases, it is the gift giver who is liable for any gift taxes, rather than the recipient.

Also, to be considered a gift for tax purposes, the gift must be irrevocable, which means you can't take it back. Gifts to adults generally must be what's called a "present interest," which means that the recipient has unfettered access to the money now. (Gifts to trusts for minors, however, are generally an exception—the money is held in trust until the children reach adulthood.) And if you die within three years of making a taxable gift, the money is considered part of your estate. That's to prevent you from making large deathbed gifts to avoid the possibility of estate taxes.

## PROS AND CONS OF GIVING WHILE LIVING

Because you're giving up the money for good, many people are justifiably concerned about making gifts while they are still alive, because they are worried they might eventually need the money. So before making any large gifts while alive, consider whether you are properly covered for retirement, health care and long-term care. Understandably, many people would rather their estates owe taxes after death than run out of money during their lifetime.

There are plenty of benefits to making gifts—especially non-taxable gifts under the $13,000 annual gift tax exclusion—during your lifetime. For one, your beneficiaries might have more need for the money now, when they are younger, perhaps for college or a down payment on a first home. Making gifts also reduces the size of your estate, minimizing the possibility of estate taxes. And if you make gifts of assets that are depressed in value, such as shares of stock that have gone down, they can appreciate outside of your estate, with your heirs reaping the benefits.

The current tax laws provide another advantage for giving while living. Many states impose state estate taxes and have much stingier state exemptions than the $5 million federal exemption. (New York, for instance, imposes state estate taxes on estates over $1 million.) So these days, to reduce possible state estate taxes, it may make sense to give your heirs funds during your lifetime, rather than leaving them the money at your death. (As of this writing, only two states impose state gift taxes.)

Unlike many complex tax savings strategies, some gift-giving tactics, such as making annual gifts under the exclusion, are quite simple and don't involve pricey legal fees or consultations. Plus you can see the beneficiaries of your gifts enjoy them. And a lifetime gift can help you determine whether an heir can responsibly handle money if he or she receives a large windfall upon your death.

Note, though, that gifts made during your lifetime don't

receive a step-up in basis, unlike assets left in your estate. So if you make gifts while living, your original cost basis carries over to your recipient. That means that if your recipient sells the asset, he or she might owe hefty capital gains taxes. But if the asset is bequeathed to your heir in your estate, its cost basis rises to full market value at death.

So if you bought a stock for $1,000 ages ago that is now worth $15,000 and you give it to your daughter, her capital gains on a sale would be measured from the $1,000 purchase price, rather than from the value on the date of the gift. But if you bequeath the stock to her upon your death, her cost basis would jump to the full market value on the date of your death, which means that your daughter would owe less in capital gains taxes.

Giving away large portions of your estate could also cause problems if you later seek to qualify for Medicaid, the federal-state program that covers health care for the poor and which is the nation's chief source of funding for nursing home care for seniors. Legislation passed in 2006 placed limits on how much seniors can transfer to others, in order to become eligible for Medicaid-paid nursing home care. If you make significant gifts during the five years before applying for Medicaid long-term-care coverage, you may have trouble qualifying for the benefits.

Also beware that making gifts could cause problems for your beneficiaries, such as students applying for college financial aid, or for senior citizens, whose Social Security benefits could become subject to taxes or tax increases.

And it's smart to consider the emotional issues of making lifetime gifts. Are you comfortable parting with an asset that you may have worked a lifetime to build? Could your gift negatively (or positively) affect your recipient?

## SMART GIFT-GIVING STRATEGIES

Making annual gifts to your heirs below the annual gift tax exclusion is a simple but effective way to transfer money to your heirs while reducing the amount of money subject to the estate tax.

It's important to note that non-cash gifts may also be subject to tax if valuable enough. If you give away things such as art or collectibles, make sure to get them properly appraised, in writing, by a professional appraiser, if you're worried such gifts might go over the $13,000 threshold (the exemption in 2011). Treating your extended family to a luxurious vacation may also count as a gift for tax purposes. Giving, rather than selling, appreciated assets, such as shares of stock that have gone up in value, can also move money out of your estate, while also avoiding capital gains taxes. (However, as discussed previously, one drawback of giving away appreciated assets while living is that your heirs can't benefit from the step-up in tax basis at your death.)

In addition to making outright gifts to children, grandchildren or anyone else you choose, you can make gifts to irrevocable trusts set up for your family, or to Uniform Gifts to Minors Act (UGMA) accounts for minor children or grandchildren. (Note that if you're the custodian of the UGMA accounts, the money will be counted as part of your estate, so make sure you're not the account custodian.) To fund these accounts and to avoid gift taxes, many people make gifts up to the amount of the annual exclusion ($13,000 per recipient, for unlimited recipients, in 2011).

## TUITION AND MEDICAL EXPENSES

Another smart strategy to pass money to your heirs: you can directly pay family members' tuition and medical bills without incurring any gift taxes. It doesn't count against that annual exclusion if you pay for someone else's tuition or medical expenses, no matter how large your payments may be—as long as those payments are made directly to the educational institution or medical services provider. Thus, you can move large amounts of money out of your estate tax-free, without even

## PREPAYING TUITION

You can also cut your tax bill by prepaying multiple years of family members' tuition bills. Let's say your grandson is about to start kindergarten at an elite K–5 private school. You can directly pay the school all six years of your grandson's tuition, even though he is only a kindergartener.

Tax advisers say this technique, which has been bolstered by an IRS ruling, could be a smart move for people with large estates who want to pay for a student's tuition and fear they might not live long enough to pay the bills as they come due each year. This way, they can help their families deal with soaring education costs—private school tuition at certain elite schools can run some $30,000 a year, and college tuition can cost far more—and skirt hefty federal estate and gift taxes.

Prepaying tuition for multiple years can move a large amount of money out of your estate—reducing possible estate tax bills—while still leaving the annual gift tax exclusion open to make other gifts. It's also a simple method; there's no need to hire a lawyer to draft complex trust or other sophisticated wealth transfer techniques.

But there are some risks. To pass muster with the IRS, tax experts recommend that the gifts to the school be nonrefundable. But the child may refuse to attend the school, transfer out, get expelled or drop out—which means you could be out of luck if you've already prepaid his or her tuition. The tactic is best suited for those who are concerned they might not live long enough to pay each year's tuition as it comes up, can afford to part with the money permanently, are comfortable the child will complete education at that school and are willing for the school to keep the money in any event.

There are other tax-efficient tuition alternatives, including simply directly paying annual tuition costs each year or funding a 529 college savings plan.

having to report your gifts to the IRS—and without eating into any of your estate tax or lifetime gift tax amounts.

One way to make direct tuition or medical payments without having to deal with lots of bills or check writing is to use what's called an "agency account." Let's say you want to fund a private school education for your grandson (your daughter's son). To use an agency account, you open and fund a bank account, but give your daughter a power of attorney that allows her to make tuition or medical payments from the account for your grandson's benefit.

## 529 COLLEGE SAVINGS PLANS

So-called 529 plans, named after a section of the tax code, allow family members to save for students' tuition at college or graduate school. Contributions are made with after-tax dollars and the accounts grow tax-deferred; distributions aren't subject to federal income tax if they are used for school expenses. Many states also offer state tax deductions to residents who use in-state plans. (A great resource on 529 plans is www.savingforcollege.com.)

However, unlike making direct tuition payments to a college, contributions to 529 plans are treated as gifts to the named beneficiary of the plan. Under 2011 law, you can give up to $13,000 a year tax-free per 529 plan beneficiary, which means you can move a lot of money out of your estate if you have lots of children or grandkids with 529 plans.

What's more, you can front-load a 529 plan by making up to five years' worth of payments at once. That means in 2011, you could give up to $65,000 to a 529 plan at once, moving a large chunk of money out of your estate. But if you die before the five years are up, a portion of the gift—the contributions for the years that have not yet occurred—may go back into your estate.

Another unusual benefit of a gift to a 529 plan: unlike most gifts, it is revocable. That's good news for those who are worried that if the unexpected occurs, they might need the money back. You can take back your contributions from a 529 plan if needed. But, of course, if you later take back the money, its value goes right back into your estate—nullifying any estate tax benefits.

## THE GENERATION-SKIPPING TRANSFER TAX

For those who want their estate plans to largely benefit their grandchildren or great-grandchildren, take note: there's another tax to consider. This is called the "generation-skipping transfer tax," or GST tax.

If you transfer large amounts of money to a relative more than one generation below you (such as your grandkids) or to an unrelated person more than 37½ years younger than you, or even to a *trust* benefitting grandkids, you might be subject to the GST tax.

Luckily, there's a GST tax exemption, which in 2011 was a large $5 million per individual (or $10 million for a married couple transferring assets). However, if you transfer amounts over the exemption to grandchildren, great-grandchildren or beyond, the GST tax, which has a top rate of 35% in 2011, is levied *on top* of any estate or gift taxes you might owe. (Bequests to grandchildren whose parents died before the transfer aren't subject to the GST tax.)

As I've discussed, the estate, generation-skipping and gift taxes all have the same $5 million exemption in 2011 (indexed for inflation in 2012). Note that whatever bequests or large gifts you make to grandchildren or other skipped generations reduce the amount of your estate tax exemption. So if you leave $4 million to a generation-skipping trust for your grandchildren at death, then only $1 million would be left in your estate for other heirs free of estate tax. In order to let the IRS know you're using part or all of your $5 million exemption for grandchildren or other skipped generations, you typically make a GST election on your gift and estate tax returns. (Your lawyer or tax adviser should help you do this.)

Also be aware that, unlike the estate tax exemption, the generation-skipping exemption is *not* portable between spouses under current law. So let's say that there's only $1 million in my estate left after that $4 million bequest to a generation-skipping trust. Once I die, the remaining $1 million left in my exemption is portable for estate-tax purposes and carries over to my husband, who can shield $6 million of assets from estate taxes. However, he can only use $5 million to shelter generation-skipping taxes, because the GST exemption is not portable between spouses.

Some families use what are called "dynasty trusts" or generation-skipping trusts to take advantage of the GST exemption and to keep more money in the family to benefit future generations. In a typical dynasty trust, a grandparent transfers assets to the trust without going over the GST exemption ($5 million per individual in 2011). Many families fund these trusts by making tax-free annual gifts below the annual gift tax exclusion ($13,000 in 2011). The trust holds and invests the money for beneficiaries—grandchildren, great-grandchildren and beyond. You can design it so that trust distributions go to children or grandchildren while the principal stays in the trust—in some cases for decades. If the trust was funded with amounts below the generation-skipping, estate or gift tax exemptions, any appreciation is free of those transfer taxes. As long as money stays in the trust, it can pass from generation to generation without additional generation-skipping taxes, allowing the trust to accumulate vast sums over time. (See Chapter Five for more information on dynasty trusts.)

The GST tax—and the GST tax exemption—are extremely complex, and some very wealthy families have gotten caught in GST-planning traps. Therefore, I strongly advise seeking the counsel of an estate or tax lawyer if you think you might have an estate large enough to be subject to the GST

## WHEN A SPOUSE IS NOT A U.S. CITIZEN

Established estate-planning rules get thrown out the window when dealing with spouses or family members who are not U.S. citizens.

For instance, husbands and wives who are both U.S. citizens can give unlimited amounts of money to each other either during life or at death, without being subject to gift or estate taxes. But gifts to a spouse who is not a U.S. citizen are subject to an annual limit, which is indexed for inflation (in 2011 it was $134,000).

Unless you set up a special trust, you can't leave money over the amount of the individual estate tax exemption to a non-citizen spouse free of estate taxes. That's because the government is worried that your surviving spouse could flee the country after you die, without Uncle Sam getting the chance to tax it.

What should international couples do? One solution, of course, is for the non-citizen spouse to become a U.S. citizen. But if that's not in the cards—and if you expect your combined estate to exceed the amount of the estate tax exemption—you can set up a special trust called a "qualified domestic trust," or a QDOT, which meets all sorts of detailed requirements laid out by the government.

The trust doesn't avoid taxes completely: it defers any estate taxes until the death of the non-citizen spouse. QDOTs must follow lots of complex rules, so make sure to consult a qualified lawyer if you might need one.

tax. This is not an area where you want to go it alone, without the advice of experts who know the particulars of your situation.

## FAMILY LOANS: THE BANK OF MOM AND DAD

One wealth transfer alternative to making a gift is to make a loan instead. Loans can be a good idea if you want to pass on an amount greater than either the annual gift exclusion or the lifetime gift exemption. But you can't give relatives a ton of money and simply call it a loan to avoid gift taxes; the loan has to be a real loan, interest and all, with the expectation that the money will indeed be paid back on schedule.

The IRS allows relatives to lend money to one another at a special interest rate, typically well below standard bank rates, called the "applicable federal rate" (AFR), which is set monthly by the government. (There are short-term, mid-term and long-term AFRs for different loan terms.)

Intra-family loans are attractive because of their low interest rates—and are also particularly appealing during economic downturns if banks tighten lending. But loans can also be a smart estate-planning strategy. If you loan money to your daughter and she invests wisely with the proceeds, she may have extra money left over after repaying you.

My husband and I used a family mortgage when we bought our first house several years ago. It's a typical thirty-year mortgage, except the money was lent to us by a relative's trust (trusts can also make loans) at a rate several percentage points lower than bank rates at the time. We saved a bunch of money because of the low rate and because we avoided hefty bank mortgage and closing fees. We make monthly payments, just as we would in a typical mortgage, except the money goes to our relative's trust rather than to the bank.

Family loans should be done carefully, in writing, with the help of an estate lawyer or tax adviser, to make sure they'll pass muster with the IRS. In the agreement, state the principal amount, the interest rate, the length of the loan and whether payments are due annually, semiannually, quarterly or monthly.

## FAMILY LIMITED PARTNERSHIPS

One strategy that has allowed thousands of parents to pass large sums of money to their children virtually tax-free is the family limited partnership. They are controversial, though, because they have been challenged by the IRS in numerous court cases, although the strategy is legal if done carefully.

Family limited partnerships are designed to curb estate and gift taxes by moving assets out of someone's estate and into a partnership. A parent transfers business or investment assets—usually a family business, real estate or securities—to a partnership formed with his or her children; then most of the shares in the partnerships are given to the kids.

Parents, however, can retain a small ownership stake and are sometimes general partners, which means they can make management and investment decisions. The kids typically are limited partners, with less control. Because of this limited control, the value of the children's shares can often be discounted by 20% to 40%, thereby lowering the gift tax bite. The upshot: the parents can still manage the assets while avoiding hefty estate and gift taxes.

For years, the IRS has challenged family limited partnerships, but the structures, when executed properly, have generally held up in court. The partnerships have other benefits, too, such as asset protection; the money held by the partnership is tough for creditors to reach without a court order.

Many estate planners say that family limited partnerships can still be kosher if structured correctly. Lawyers say that partnerships should have a valid non-tax-related reason to exist, such as to pool investment assets, including stock or commercial real estate, or to manage an existing family business. To avoid IRS scrutiny, you should set up a partnership while you're in good health, rather than, say, on your deathbed, and create a separate bank account for the structure. Also, don't transfer personal assets, such as your primary residence or furniture, into the partnership, and avoid using partnership assets to pay rent or medical expenses. Instead, distribute income to partners when the partnership assets perform well, and pay partners according to their ownership stake.

Partnerships are more likely to be upheld if the children also donate assets to the partnership. And parents should consider reducing control over the partnership by naming an independent third party, such as a bank, as the general partner. While that means parents would have less control over the assets, it also means the partnership is more likely to withstand IRS scrutiny.

Family limited partnerships don't come cheap, however. They can cost anywhere from about $5,000 to $30,000 in lawyers' and appraisal fees to set up, and as much as several thousand dollars a year in accounting fees. There's also a similar structure, called a "family limited liability company"; certain states have laws and tax codes that might make an LLC more appealing than a partnership.

## CHAPTER 3

# WILLS: PASSING ON YOUR PROPERTY

## CREATING A WILL

A will is the centerpiece of most estate plans. This legal document allows you to control who receives your assets and property after you die, to thoughtfully manage the transfer of your property in an orderly fashion and to take into consideration the special needs and situations of your heirs.

If you don't have a will and die intestate, as I explained in Chapter One, state law decides for you. That means your money and possessions might not end up where you would wish.

A will is also the document in which you can name guardians you wish to care for your minor children if you are unable to do so. In a will you can even set up trusts to benefit heirs that go into effect upon your death, called testamentary trusts. (I'll discuss guardianship in more detail in Chapter Eight and trusts in Chapter Five.) You'll also name an executor, who administers the estate after your death and distributes your property, among other duties.

A will is "revocable," which means you can change its provisions—who gets what—at any point during your lifetime. The most recent version of your will supersedes prior versions, so make sure that any new version or amendment is clearly dated.

When drawing up a will, you should consider some of the following issues:

- Whom do you want to receive your property after your death—and do you want them to get that property outright or in a trust?

- Do you want to leave your property equally to all of your children?

- Do you want to bequeath assets to other heirs, such as grandchildren, siblings or friends?

- Do you want to leave anything to charity?

- Do you want certain tangible items, such as a piece of jewelry or a painting, to go to specific family members?

- Are there certain family heirlooms, or a family home, you don't want to be sold?

- Whom do you want to name as an executor?

- Whom do you want to name as guardians for your minor children?

There are some basic guidelines you should follow when drafting a will. These apply whether you seek the guidance of an estate-planning lawyer or choose the do-it-yourself route (advisable only if you have a simple family and economic situation).

- You should clearly identify yourself by your full legal name as the person creating the will.

WILLS: PASSING ON YOUR PROPERTY

- State that this will voids any previous wills you have made. (Any ambiguity will leave it open to legal challenges.)

- The will should not be handwritten but typed and printed.

- The will should be signed and dated in the presence of witnesses.

Note, however, that witnessing requirements, such as the number of witnesses, vary from state to state. In some states, for instance, beneficiaries of the will can't serves as witnesses, so make sure you are familiar with the rules in your state, especially if you don't use a lawyer.

It's smart to be as specific as possible when spelling out your wishes, to avoid misinterpretations—and future fights—among heirs. Many wills, for instance, neglect to include a list of personal property, leaving heirs to fight among themselves for Grandma's silver. (I'll go over some smart strategies to give away your personal property in Chapter Nine.)

If you opt to leave the bulk of your assets to a primary beneficiary, such as a spouse, you should also name successor beneficiaries, such as children, grandchildren, friends or charities, in case your primary beneficiary dies before you do. For instance, I specified in my will that my husband is my primary beneficiary and my children are successor beneficiaries. This way, if my husband dies before I do (and I neglect to adjust my will), my assets would then go to my kids. I've also named my siblings to be successor beneficiaries after my children, which means my siblings would receive my assets if both my husband and my kids pass away.

In addition, if you're married, you'll need to consider your obligations to your spouse. State laws, which vary, typically protect surviving spouses from being disinherited, unless spouses sign special waivers or contractual agreements. If you

## SIMULTANEOUS DEATH

What happens if you and your spouse both die simultaneously, such as in a fatal car accident? Under the Uniform Simultaneous Death Act, adopted in some form by each state, your assets are transferred as if you survived your spouse and vice versa. So that means your property goes to your successor beneficiaries and your spouse's property goes to his or her successor beneficiaries. To be on the safe side, many lawyers also include a simultaneous death clause in the will, stating this explicitly.

don't leave enough for your spouse under state law requirements, he or she may still be able to receive more.

## YOURS, MINE AND OURS: OWNERSHIP AND COMMUNITY PROPERTY

When creating a will, you'll first need to figure out who legally owns the assets that you enjoy—your home, your savings account, stocks and so on. Are they owned by you, your spouse or both jointly—or by another entity, such as a trust or partnership? When you're married, it can be all too easy to forget which assets are in whose name, but it's key to determine ownership, so that the appropriate owners can specify how their assets are to be handled.

Determining ownership—and doing some advance planning—can be especially important when it comes to housing. If your spouse or partner solely owns the home that you live in together, it's possible you could be kicked out after his or her death, unless you make advance arrangements, such as provisions in his or her will, letting you stay there.

Ownership might seem like a simple thing to determine, but state laws can complicate things. Certain states have special rules because they are "community property" states: Arizona, California, Idaho, Louisiana, Nevada, New Mexico, Texas, Washington and Wisconsin. (In Alaska, couples can opt in to community property rules through a special agreement or trust.)

If you live in a community property state, any property acquired or income earned during marriage is considered to be jointly owned equally by you and your spouse. (An exception: gifts or inheritances received during marriage are generally considered individual property, although the investment income or appreciation from such gifts or inheritances may not be.) Property owned separately before marriage is also generally exempt from community property.

For estate-planning purposes, half of all the community property is considered your spouse's, but you're free to do whatever you want with your half of the community property. Couples may be able to get around community property rules through special prenuptial or postnuptial agreements waiving community property, or by including spousal waivers in estate planning documents.

Community property can have advantages for estate-planning purposes. For instance, when one spouse in a community property state dies, *both* spouses' shares of the property receive a step-up in cost basis. (As I discussed in the previous chapter, the cost basis is the original value of an asset—either the original purchase price or, when inherited, the value of the shares upon the original owner's death—used to determine capital gains or losses for tax purposes when the asset is eventually sold.)

Let's say a husband and wife who live in a community property state own a home that they bought for $100,000 and which is now worth $400,000 at the husband's death. Under community property rules, only half of the home is considered to be part of his estate. But the cost basis rises for the *entire* house, even his wife's portion. So if the wife sells the house, her cost basis is now $400,000 (rather than $100,000, the original purchase price) and she would owe no capital gains taxes upon the sale. By contrast, if the couple lived in a separate property state, only the husband's half of the house would get the step-up in cost basis; the wife's half would still have a cost basis of $100,000 for tax purposes, which means she would still owe hefty capital gains taxes if she sold the house upon her husband's death.

If you live in a community property state, make sure to contact a lawyer familiar with state laws, since rules can get complicated, especially when it comes to estate taxes.

What if you live in one of the majority of states that don't have community property? Your spouse still is entitled to some portion of your estate under state law—although not necessarily the automatic one-half portion in community property states. This portion that your spouse is entitled to is called a "spousal elective share" and varies from state to state, sometimes depending on how long you were married. If you and your spouse create a prenuptial or postnuptial contract, though, you may be able to waive the spousal elective share.

## NAMING AN EXECUTOR

Being an executor is not a job for slackers. The role involves gathering and taking inventory of the estate's assets, handling any debts or taxes owed by the estate or the decedent and, if necessary, representing the estate in any legal claims (with the help of a lawyer).

The executor will have to file the deceased's will in the local probate court, notify any beneficiaries and distribute the estate's remaining property to beneficiaries. The executor has to file federal and state estate tax returns, typically within nine months of the death (or fifteen months with an extension), if the estate's gross value exceeds any estate tax exemptions. And under the new estate tax rules for 2011 and 2012, if you want any of your unused federal estate tax exemption to carry over to your surviving spouse, the executor must still file a federal estate tax return for that to happen—even if you don't expect to owe any tax at all.

## TILL DEBT DO US PART?

What happens to any debts, such as a mortgage or credit card balance, that you may owe creditors when you die? Will your heirs be on the hook to pay the debt in full, even out of their own pockets?

Unfortunately, there aren't really clear-cut answers to these questions. How an estate's debt is handled is based on many factors, especially state laws. If your estate doesn't have enough money to pay all of your debts, state law determines which creditors must be paid first and which ones must be paid in full, in part or not at all.

Some loans, such as many mortgages or car loans, may be passed along with the property they accompany. So if your children inherit a house or a car, in some cases they may be liable for its mortgage or loan, too. (If they don't want to assume the debt, they can choose to refuse, or disclaim, the inheritance, as we'll discuss later on.)

In many cases, debts are paid out of the assets in the estate by selling off large pieces of property such as a house. Certain loans, though, may be forgiven at death, such as federal college loans. (An estate may still be liable for private student loans, however.) And if there isn't enough in the estate to cover the remaining debts, many will simply remain unpaid, depending on state law.

Beware, though, that under Medicaid estate recovery rules, states may go after some estates for repayment of certain Medicaid benefits. If you or your spouse is a Medicaid recipient, it's important to check with an estate or elder law attorney about your state's rules.

If you are an heir or executor of an estate with debt, or you expect your own estate to owe money, consult a lawyer who is familiar with your own state's laws, in order to know what the estate or heirs may be on the hook for where you live. If you are concerned that your estate might be debt-ridden, you might consider buying life insurance to help provide more liquidity to your estate.

What's more, the executor has to make sure the decedent's home, if empty, is secure; sell or distribute any remaining assets; and make sure to receive all correspondence, such as bills. And those are only some of the responsibilities! (However, the executor can certainly hire a lawyer, accountant or other advisers for help.)

In sum, naming an executor is not a decision to take lightly. Make sure you name someone who is responsible and trustworthy—and, of course, name successor executors in case your first pick is unable to fulfill the duties. If you don't name an executor for your will, the probate court will appoint one for you.

Many people name a family member or close friend, while others name a trusted adviser, such as a lawyer or accountant, or even a financial services institution to serve in the role. Some families prefer the impartiality of someone outside the family, who can dole out family heirlooms without emotional ties. Others would actually rather that someone connected to the family take on such a critical task, under the assumption that he or she may be willing to spend more time on the duties and may be more likely to act in the family's interests. You can also name co-executors, who share the duty. Think twice before naming someone who lives far away to be an executor, though, because a long-distance executor can slow down the process.

Executors are entitled to payment for fulfilling the role (states typically set fee limits), although some executors waive the payments if they are close relatives or friends.

## FAIR DOESN'T ALWAYS MEAN EQUAL

One of the toughest questions parents face when drawing up a will is how much to leave for their children—and whether they should leave an equal share to each child.

Families take into account many different factors when determining how to distribute property. No two members of a family are exactly alike, and thus distributions may not be,

## PER STIRPES VS. PER CAPITA

When you're leaving assets in your will, you can choose to simply leave the assets "per stirpes" or "per capita."

What does this mean? Let's say you have a son and daughter. Your son has two children and your daughter has none.

"Per stirpes" means, essentially, dividing your estate by family lines. Let's say your son dies before you do. If you left all of your assets per stirpes, half of your money will go to your son's two children, and the other half will go to your daughter. The money is split equally between your two children's branches of the family, even if they have different numbers of kids themselves.

On the other hand, if you leave your assets in equal shares per capita, the money is divided equally per person, so that each surviving descendant gets an equal share of the money. That means that each of your two surviving grandchildren and your daughter get a third of your inheritance.

Every family structure is different, and for some families, per stirpes is more suitable than per capita, and vice versa. If you don't want to use either, you can specifically name who should receive property, in what order (if someone predeceases you) and in what share. The website www.mystatewill.com has handy per stirpes and per capita calculators to help you determine how much your heirs would receive under each method.

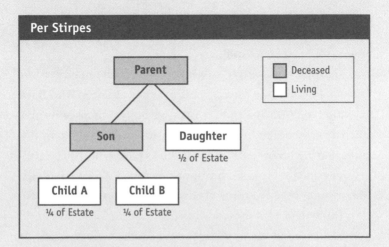

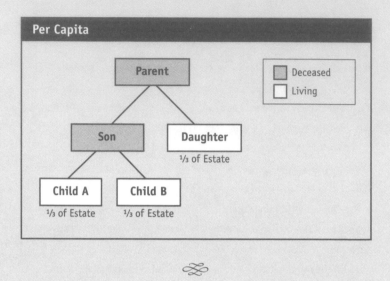

either. One child may be far more successful financially than another. One child may have six children of his own, while another may have just one child. A son or daughter may take full-time care of your ailing spouse, while another child rarely visits or calls. You may have a close, loving relationship with one son or daughter, and be estranged from another. Things can get even more complicated when you are dealing with a family business; I'll go over some business succession strategies in Chapter Six. The take-home message: what's fair may not result in an equal split.

Many parents want to support children who need greater financial help, while others want to repay children who have provided important support or caregiving. Some parents may have already helped one child considerably more than another during his or her lifetime, such as paying for pricey grad school education or providing money for a down payment. Meanwhile, other parents are reluctant to reward a particularly difficult or problematic child.

As I'll discuss further here and in even more detail in Chapter Nine, if you do choose to support children unevenly,

## HOW TO DISINHERIT SOMEONE

You and your son are no longer on speaking terms. When you last did your will, you left a good portion of your estate to him. Now you want to change that. How should you go about either disinheriting him or leaving him dramatically less than other family members?

It's often tougher than it sounds. Many state laws protect close family members, especially spouses, from being left out entirely. In most cases you can't completely disinherit your spouse unless the spouse agrees in a legal contract to be disinherited, or unless your husband or wife has abandoned you. As noted, in the community property states, your spouse is actually entitled to half of your joint property or half of what you earned or acquired during marriage. And in some places, children may have rights to a piece, too.

The bottom line: check with a lawyer in your state so that you are not breaking any rules if you want to disinherit someone. Otherwise, your estate is ripe for many legal challenges from disgruntled, disinherited relatives.

To help deter lawsuits from disinherited relatives, there are some other steps you should take. For one, make sure you clearly name the disinherited relative in your will or trust and state that he or she gets nothing. Some lawyers also suggest that you write a letter to accompany the will stating the reasons why you chose to shut out your heir.

Real estate heiress Leona Helmsley, for example, in her will left nothing to two of her four grandchildren, but left $5 million each to the other two, as well as $12 million to her Maltese dog, Trouble. The will stated, "I have not made any provisions in this Will for my grandson CRAIG PANZIRER or my granddaughter MEEGAN PANZIRER for reasons which are known to them." (A New York judge later reduced the amount left to Trouble to $2 million.)

※

there are steps you can take to help protect your will against challenges, including proving your capacity and writing extra letters of instruction.

Some estate lawyers suggest adding a statement in your will explaining the disparity, especially if you choose to give uneven bequests purely because of your beneficiaries' financial situation, not their behavior. Paramus, New Jersey, estate lawyer Martin Shenkman, for instance, suggests adding a statement to the effect of: "I have made a larger bequest to my son Sam, out of consideration for his greater financial needs, and not in any way to indicate greater love or affection for him than for my other children."

Although such a statement may sound corny, Shenkman adds, many heirs "equate love and money." Explicitly saying that's not the case, even if you think it's obvious, "can take the sting out of unequal bequests," he says.

You can also support less wealthy children in ways that won't show up in your will and thereby are less likely to be challenged after your death. One way is to support children while you are living, rather than after your death. You can make annual gifts, as I discussed in the previous chapter, including gifts to 529 college savings plans, or by paying directly for their health care or tuition.

To reimburse children who provide important care for you or your spouse, you can even draw up a caregiving contract and pay children for their caregiving duties. (I'll discuss these arrangements in more depth at the end of Chapter Nine.)

You can also buy a life insurance policy, naming a less wealthy child as the owner and beneficiary, or an annuity, which can ensure a stream of cash over time during the child's lifetime. (I'll go over annuities in more detail in Chapter Six.)

But be careful when making uneven bequests because of your kids' differing financial situations. As you well know, financial fortunes can change quickly, so your very wealthy child who you think might not need your support might eventually end up losing his or her fortune. Meanwhile, the child who's now a starving artist may one day strike it rich. You also want to be wary of penalizing children who are prosperous, such as a hardworking surgeon, by leaving them fewer assets than other less financially successful children.

One solution suggested by estate planners is to split, say, 75% to 80% of your assets equally among your children, while leaving the remaining 20% to 25% of your assets in a trust for your children's emergency needs. You will, however, want to name an independent trustee (such as another relative, a friend or a financial services firm) to distribute funds from the trust, someone who will do so fairly and appropriately.

I'll discuss more strategies for maintaining family harmony in your estate plan in Chapter Nine.

## ETHICAL WILLS

While I highly recommend face-to-face conversations about estate plans with family members or other heirs, some people find it easier to put the reasons behind their estate-planning decisions on paper. They choose to write letters or make videos expressing their values or their hopes and dreams for their heirs, in what are often termed "ethical wills."

These are not legal documents, like typical wills, but they are a good way for you to let your heirs know what's important to you philosophically, rather than just materially. Some families even choose to share them with their heirs while they are still alive, rather than after they have passed away.

Ethical wills can also help you clarify certain estate-planning decisions, such as giving your heirs unequal inheritances or even disinheriting someone. Writing your wishes in a letter or stating them in a video that accompanies your more formal estate-planning documents is an effective way to help prevent misinterpretations or, worse, estate battles.

## DISCLAIMING AN INHERITANCE: WHEN IT MAKES SENSE TO SAY NO

Saying no to an inheritance may sound crazy, but advisers note there may be good reasons for your heirs to decline—or "disclaim," in legal jargon—all or part of a windfall. The tactic allows your heirs to make decisions based on their financial situation and tax laws at the time they receive their inheritance, rather than when you made your estate plans.

Why would your heirs want to disclaim an inheritance? One reason is that an inheritance could cause your kids' estates to be subject to federal or state estate taxes, so it might make sense for them to disclaim if they don't need the money.

Beware that the tax code sets out strict rules for disclaiming property. That means some advance planning is important if you want to provide your heirs the option to disclaim after you pass away. For one thing, your heirs cannot direct where the money goes after they disclaim it. Instead, you must specify in your will who gets what when assets are disclaimed. (These are sometimes called "disclaimer provisions.") So, for instance, if your son chooses to disclaim his inheritance, your will can specify that the money goes to a family trust or charitable foundation instead.

Also, heirs must disclaim any wealth in writing within nine months of the death. They are not allowed to use the assets if they are planning on disclaiming them. That means they cannot cash a dividend check if they want to disclaim stock, for instance.

James Lange, a Pittsburgh attorney, has drafted hundreds of wills with disclaimer provisions. Many of the wills contain a so-called cascading beneficiary plan, with provisions allowing a spouse to send assets into trusts for the children, and also letting children send assets into trusts for the grandchildren. Using this sequence of disclaimers, assets are moved out of the older generation's estate and to a generation that often is in a lower tax bracket. He creates flow charts for clients showing how the money would pass if the disclaimers are activated.

One of his clients, a professor, drafted a will with a cascading beneficiary plan. In the event of his death, his wife can choose to disclaim a portion of their estate in favor of their two children. One or both of the professor's sons, in turn, could choose to further disclaim some assets in favor of their own kids. Of course, the client's spouse or children could decide not to disclaim and keep all of the money for themselves.

Disclaimer provisions in wills aren't without their problems. Because heirs have to make a quick decision about whether to keep the money or give it to someone else, families are forced to deal with a complex financial issue at a time when grief may make such a decision particularly difficult. And unlike other wills that set aside specific inheritances for children, married couples have to trust that the surviving spouse will give the children their fair share. (This can be a problem in some second marriages.)

Another of Lange's clients chose not to disclaim any of her $3 million inheritance after her husband died, in order to benefit her own children. "She said, 'I want it all,' " said Lange. "Had I picked up on the fact that she was going to act that way, I probably wouldn't have suggested it."

## CHAPTER 4

# PROBATE
# AND WAYS TO
# AVOID IT

## WHAT A WILL DOESN'T COVER:
## PROBATE AND NON-PROBATE PROPERTY

Having a will is incredibly important. But take note that some big assets aren't governed by the terms of your will. In this chapter, I'll discuss property that can be transferred outside of a will, avoiding probate, the public process by which a court validates a will.

There are two kinds of property: probate and non-probate. Probate property is transferred to your heirs via your will, through the court-supervised probate process, which can be both costly and time-consuming (though the degree depends on where you live, since probate procedures vary widely by state).

Meanwhile, non-probate property passes directly to your heirs without going through probate and is not governed by the terms of your will.

Non-probate property generally includes accounts that have beneficiary designations, such as retirement plans, insurance policies, annuities and accounts that are designated "payable on death" or "transfer on death"; certain accounts or property that you own jointly with someone else; and property held in a trust created during your lifetime.

By rearranging how your property is titled, much of your estate can sidestep probate and go directly to your heirs. For instance, your savings accounts, brokerage accounts and mutual funds can pass to your heirs without probate if you title the accounts as "payable on death" or "transfer on death." And upon your death, assets in a living trust avoid probate and go directly to beneficiaries.

Note that avoiding probate doesn't mean avoiding estate taxes. In fact, using joint accounts and payable-on-death accounts can sometimes make it tougher to employ certain estate-planning tactics designed to trim taxes.

And bear in mind that even if many of your assets are titled to avoid probate, you'll still need a will, too. There will always be some assets that won't pass directly to your heirs, and a will dictates how they should be transferred.

## WHAT IS PROBATE?

After a death, a will goes through probate, the legal process of administering an estate. Probate is designed to protect the rights of beneficiaries and creditors and to help ensure an orderly transfer of your property. One of your executor's chief duties is to see your will through the probate process.

The probate process varies drastically by state. In some places, probate is relatively quick and inexpensive, but in other states there are large probate court filing fees and substantial delays. So before you make drastic moves to retitle your assets or set up a special trust, talk to your lawyer about probate in your state. Also, if you own real estate in more than one state, your executor may have to deal with probate proceedings in multiple locations.

Regardless of where you live, probate has some unavoidable downsides. Your estate will likely incur legal fees to file your will in probate court. Probate is also not a private process;

in general, the contents of your will are part of the public record, which means that your family's finances and affairs may
be on display. And if your will is challenged by disgruntled
heirs, that can add heavy legal costs, as well as time and uncer-
tainty, to the process.

## JOINT OWNERSHIP WITH RIGHTS OF SURVIVORSHIP

As I discussed earlier, how you own your property has a big effect on how you can pass it on to others. If you own the asset by
yourself, you can do with it what you please. Things get more
complicated, however, when assets are owned jointly.

One popular way of owning financial accounts or real estate is called joint ownership, or "joint tenancy, with rights of
survivorship." This means that the property is co-owned with
another person and can automatically be transferred to the
co-owner, such as a spouse or a child, when you die. The transfer of this property is not dictated by a will; instead the assets
go directly to your joint owner, sidestepping probate.

Holding property as a joint owner or tenant with rights of
survivorship is attractive because it's a very simple way to avoid
probate on the death of the first owner. However, there are a
number of downsides to such ownership, so think twice before
rushing to title much of your property in this fashion.

First of all, such ownership just delays probate, rather than
avoiding it altogether. You can skip probate on the death of
the first owner, but the property still may need to go through
probate when the surviving owner dies, if the survivor has a
sole interest in the property.

Also beware that owning property jointly may have some
negative tax consequences and may not be as flexible as some
other estate-planning tactics. For instance, if you want to add
your son as a joint tenant on a piece of real estate, you're
making a gift to him in the eyes of the IRS. Depending on
the circumstances and the size of the share, the gift could be

considered taxable. (Adding a joint owner, such as your son, to a bank account is considered a gift once your son withdraws money that he didn't deposit.)

Joint ownership also gives you less control over what your co-owner does with the property after you die. If you're worried that your co-owner could eventually mismanage the property or pass it on to someone undesirable, estate planners suggest using a trust, instead of joint ownership, to provide more control.

Another downside: your co-owner could potentially withdraw all of the assets in the account without asking you first.

So while joint ownership can be a very simple way of passing on property while minimizing probate, it can lead to some snafus. I'd suggest getting legal counsel before deciding to title a lot of your property in this way.

## ALTERNATIVES TO JOINT OWNERSHIP

- One co-ownership alternative is to have what's called "tenancy in common." This form of ownership doesn't include a right of survivorship, so each owner or tenant can sell or transfer his or her share independently. Siblings, say, might own a family vacation home as tenants in common, keeping the home in the family. One downside is that if a family feud erupts, a sibling could be free to sell his or her share to an outsider. Another caveat: if you own a tenancy-in-common share, it generally must go through probate upon your death.

- Some states allow a form of joint ownership for married couples called "tenancy by the entirety." This is very similar to joint tenancy with rights of survivorship, but it can have additional asset protection benefits, which can be helpful if a spouse is in a litigious field such as medicine.

- Yet another option is to own securities or an investment or bank account solely but have a beneficiary designation on the account, indicating that it is "transfer on death" or "payable on death," thus avoiding probate. Check with your financial institutions to see if they permit such designations on that particular asset or instrument.

## LIVING TRUSTS

An increasingly popular way to avoid probate on certain assets is to transfer them to what's called a "revocable living trust." These trusts are created while you are alive, rather than through your will. While you are living these trusts are revocable, which means that you can change them at any time, like a will.

Living trusts are not only useful to avoid probate. They are also commonly used as a way to designate someone else to manage your property if you become incapacitated and are unable to manage your own affairs. You can serve as a trustee of your living trust but name successor trustees in case you become incapacitated.

Let's say your father, a widower, goes into mental decline. Without advance planning, you or other loved ones might not be able to access his accounts unless a court rules that he is unfit and appoints someone, a guardian, to take over his finances. A living trust, however, names trustees who could take over your father's assets in the trust without going to court. (A power-of-attorney document can also provide similar benefits, as I'll discuss in Chapter Eight.)

What's more, if your father passes away, assets in the trust can pass to his heirs directly without having to go through probate. This is particularly smart for a person whose bequests might be contentious, because remember, during probate, a will's contents become part of the public record. Avoiding the publicity of probate can help shield your estate plan from potential challengers, such as disgruntled heirs.

Make sure to properly title the assets you want to be

included in the revocable living trust; if your assets aren't correctly transferred to the trust, its purpose is essentially moot. You also need to make sure you change the title of existing assets to that of the trust, as well as the titles of any big-ticket items you buy after you create the trust. (That means, for instance, that the title on John Doe's Mercedes should be registered to "the Trust of John Doe" rather than to John Doe himself.) Your estate lawyer will help you transfer your current and future assets to the trust, a process that may involve some signatures in front of a notary. You can still use the assets during your lifetime if they are owned by the revocable living trust.

It's important to stress that living trusts are not substitutes for wills. Even if you have a living trust, you still need to have a will, often called a "pour-over" will, to handle any assets that haven't been transferred into the trust, and to provide additional instructions if necessary.

Also note that revocable trusts, unlike irrevocable trusts, don't provide special tax benefits. That's because they can be changed at any time, so the assets are never considered truly out of your estate. In essence, for tax purposes, the trusts are treated as if they do not exist. That means you don't need to file a separate tax return for a revocable living trust. Instead, any trust income or losses are listed on your own tax returns.

Before setting up a revocable living trust, check with a probate lawyer in your state to make sure the cost to set up the trust doesn't exceed the likely probate fees your estate would incur without it. Also, beware of scam artists peddling what they claim are living trusts but are really high-priced annuities or else downright fraudulent.

## BENEFICIARY DESIGNATIONS

As I noted, assets with beneficiary designations are not governed by the terms of your will—and are also not subject to probate. This kind of property includes some very important assets in your estate, such as your retirement plans, including 401(k)s, IRAs and pensions; life insurance policies; annuities; and any payable-on-death or transfer-on-death bank or investment accounts.

It's crucial to fill out the beneficiary designation forms for these assets and keep them up to date to reflect new children, marriage or remarriage, divorce or the death of a beneficiary. Contact your retirement plan provider (or your employer for certain employee plans), insurer and financial services companies to get copies of these forms.

Make sure to name a primary beneficiary and a contingent beneficiary, who is a backup if your first beneficiary dies before you do. Keep your own copies of any beneficiary designation forms in a safe, secure spot. (Document storage is discussed in depth in the final chapter.)

If you name minor children as beneficiaries, they will need a guardian to manage the funds until they reach legal adulthood, usually age 18. You can also name a trust for minor children to serve as a beneficiary. (But be careful when naming a trust as a recipient of an IRA, since there are all sorts of complex rules there.)

Beneficiary designation forms can vary widely among financial institutions. Some may just ask you to name a primary and secondary beneficiary, while others may have more options, such as providing for your minor children or grandchildren, charity or a trust. It's smart to have your estate-planning adviser review your forms (especially if they are simple boilerplate ones) to make sure they properly express your wishes and mesh well with the rest of your estate plan.

Just because certain assets are governed by beneficiary designations rather than your will doesn't mean you can pass them on free of estate taxes. Retirement accounts and other assets governed by beneficiary forms may still be subject to estate taxes at your death if the amount exceeds the estate-tax exemption.

## ESTATE PLANNING WITH RETIREMENT PLANS

Estate planning can get particularly tricky when it comes to passing on the assets held in individual retirement accounts, or IRAs. In these accounts, which constitute a growing portion of many families' nest eggs, you can contribute pre-tax funds, which can grow tax-free for years. Upon reaching age 70½, though, you'll need to start taking required minimum distributions, and these withdrawals are subject to income taxes.

How your IRA is passed to your heirs is governed not by your will but instead by beneficiary designation forms provided by your IRA custodian, usually a financial services firm.

Who should you name as your IRA beneficiary? If you're like most IRA holders, you'll probably choose your surviving spouse, who can roll the money over into his or her own IRA or into a newly created one, taking required minimum distributions upon reaching age 70½.

If your surviving spouse doesn't need the money, he or she could decline the IRA altogether, in which case the IRA goes to whomever you name as your contingent beneficiaries— typically your children or your grandchildren. These beneficiaries can roll the money into what's called an "inherited IRA," which allows them to stretch out annual distributions—and defer taxes—over their own life spans. (The IRS life expectancy tables can be found at www.irs.gov.)

Purely from the standpoint of income tax deferral, it's best to leave your IRA to the youngest beneficiaries possible. The reason: the younger your beneficiaries are, the longer the IRS assumes their remaining life span to be—and the longer they can have funds grow tax-deferred in the IRA. In other words, the longer you can stretch out IRA distributions, the longer the money in the IRA can grow tax-deferred, leaving more for your heirs. Determining how much heirs need to withdraw from the IRA is subject to a number of tricky rules based on their life expectancy, so make sure they consult a tax adviser.

In practice, though, most people leave IRAs to their surviving spouses first, who are likely to need the money much sooner than children or grandchildren. And, as I said, if your surviving spouse doesn't need the money, he or she can always choose to disclaim the IRA in favor of a younger beneficiary.

As you mull over your estate plan, it's smart to let your beneficiaries know that inherited IRAs have all sorts of thorny rules and are subject to big tax bites if they mess up. Indeed, if your heirs transfer an IRA the wrong way, it can cause them to suffer painful taxes. (See the box on page 70 for more information on inheriting an IRA.)

It's important to note that unlike with most inheritances, your beneficiaries will have to pay income tax on the annual distributions they receive from the IRA they inherit. Because of the tax consequences of IRAs—they may be subject to estate taxes upon your death, and distributions are subject to income taxes for your heirs—some advisers recommend that you spend down your IRA while you are living, leaving other property to your heirs. Make sure to ask your estate advisers for guidance on IRA moves, since the accounts are subject to so many complex rules. (A list of trained IRA advisers can be found at www.irahelp.com.)

Also, avoid having your estate be the IRA beneficiary, which can lead to a big income tax hit. This can happen if you forget to name beneficiaries on your designation forms or if no one can track down the form once you pass away.

One note: if you're in a remarriage but have children from a previous one, IRA planning can be even tougher. Let's say you name your new wife as the IRA beneficiary and your kids as contingent beneficiaries. But if your wife rolls your IRA over into her own, she has the freedom to change the successor beneficiaries. She could choose to support her own children, rather than yours. If you're in a remarriage, talk to an adviser about what steps you may want to take instead. (See additional planning ideas for blended families in Chapter Nine.)

You may want to consider designating a charity as a

beneficiary of your IRA. On your beneficiary designation form, you can name a charity as a 100% beneficiary or as a partial beneficiary, naming other heirs to receive the rest of the funds. For 2011, Congress has also allowed individuals who are 70½ years old and older to directly transfer, tax-free, as much as $100,000 from their IRAs to charity. By doing so, donors can avoid paying income tax on that money, and the transfer counts toward whatever they're required to take out of their IRAs each year. (I'll discuss this tactic in more detail in Chapter Seven.)

## TRUSTS AS BENEFICIARIES

Naming a trust as the beneficiary of your IRA may be appealing to those who seek to use trusts to help minimize estate or generation-skipping taxes or protect vulnerable beneficiaries, such as a child at risk of getting a divorce or your minor grandchildren. You can put provisions in the trust that, say, prevent beneficiaries from liquidating the IRA all at once. After designating a trust as a beneficiary, you then name your heirs as beneficiaries of the trust, and they will typically receive the required minimum distributions from the trust.

Naming a trust as a beneficiary, though, is fraught with all sorts of complex tax rules. In general, to achieve the maximum income-tax-deferral benefits, trusts must follow thorny IRS guidelines called "see-through" or "conduit" trust rules, but there are all sorts of exceptions. The bottom line: before designating a trust as an IRA beneficiary on the form, make sure to consult your estate-planning lawyer, as you don't want to get caught in any unnecessary tax traps.

A similar option is to use what's called a "trusteed IRA." These IRAs operate like typical custodial IRAs, where the money is held in a bank or investment firm, but they offer certain protections of a trust. For instance, they can have special provisions to protect spendthrift children or control distributions to beneficiaries. You can, say, prevent a child from

## INHERITING AN IRA

Be *very* careful if you are lucky enough to inherit an IRA from a loved one. Make a wrong move, and it could have major tax consequences.

One Pittsburgh mediator I interviewed inherited an IRA account worth about $55,000 from his cousin several years ago. By mistake, he signed a form that liquidated the IRA all at once, which meant he owed hefty income taxes. Instead, he could have maintained the account intact and stretched out the distributions—and the taxes—over his lifetime. He realized his error only later, when he went into his accountant's office to do his taxes.

"The accountant looked at me and we all started to cry," he told me. But since the account was already liquidated, there was nothing he could do. "It was pretty disheartening."

If you inherit an IRA from your parents, grandparents or anyone other than a spouse, be careful not to roll it over into your own retirement account, and don't withdraw the money and deposit it into a new IRA. If the account is transferred or titled improperly, "boom—you'll owe tax on the whole thing," said Pittsburgh estate lawyer James Lange.

Unless the IRA belonged to your spouse (in which case more options are available) you'll want to maintain it intact and carefully retitle the IRA as an "inherited IRA," said IRA adviser Ed Slott. That makes it clear to tax authorities that the owner of the IRA died and you are the beneficiary. (For more specifics, a list of trained IRA advisers can be found at www.irahelp.com.)

Inherited IRAs are often called "stretch IRAs" because the tax benefits are stretched out for a long time. Under tax rules, you'll eventually have to take required minimum distributions from that inherited IRA. The younger you are, the smaller those required distributions will be. That means that more money can grow tax-deferred inside the IRA for many years.

cashing out the entire IRA and instead allow the trustee to make only the required annual minimum distributions, ensuring that the money grows tax-free for as long as possible. You can also specify how the assets will be invested after you pass away, ensuring investment continuity. Trusteed IRAs, however, don't have any special tax advantages over typical custodial IRAs. And financial firms tend to offer trusteed IRAs only for large accounts, often of over $1 million.

## CONSIDER THE ROTH IRA

As I just discussed, in a regular IRA, you get an up-front tax break when you put money into the account. The funds grow tax-free once inside the IRA—but you'll owe income taxes when you take required minimum distributions starting at age 70½.

The Roth IRA works differently. In a Roth IRA, you pay income taxes on your contributions, but the money grows tax-free and generally isn't taxable when you withdraw it, as long you meet certain holding requirements. (You can withdraw your direct contributions tax-free anytime; to withdraw earnings tax-free, you must be at least 59½ years old and have held the account for at least five years.)

There's also an estate-planning benefit with Roth IRAs: you're not required to take minimum annual distributions starting at age 70½, which means you can leave more funds in the account for your heirs if you don't use up all the money for your own retirement. (The money in the Roth IRA still is considered part of your estate, however, and could be subject to estate taxes if your estate is large enough.) After you die, your non-spouse Roth beneficiaries must take minimum distributions, but the money, while in the Roth, still grows tax-free, and distributions are generally still free of income tax.

One catch: you aren't allowed to contribute to a Roth IRA if your adjusted gross income exceeds a certain amount. These income limits change annually and are adjusted for inflation—in 2011, you weren't allowed to contribute to a Roth IRA if your adjusted gross income exceeded $122,000 for individuals and $179,000 for married couples filing jointly—so check with your tax adviser before you make a contribution, to make sure you are eligible. There are also limits to how much you can contribute to an IRA every year; in 2011, you could contribute up to $5,000 if you were age 49 or younger, and $6,000 if you were age 50 or older.

What about if you already have a traditional IRA or make too much money to make contributions to a Roth? Consider converting your regular IRA to a Roth IRA. That option became more attractive under new rules, effective starting in 2010, which allow anyone to make a conversion, regardless of income. In a conversion, you must pay income taxes on the money you convert—a tax adviser can help you figure out how much you'd owe—and fill out some conversion paperwork and tax forms provided by the financial services company that holds your account and your accountant. (Make sure to fill out a new beneficiary designation form, too.) The benefit is that by paying the conversion income taxes up front, you won't owe anything once you take out money from the Roth IRA.

It's important, however, to have enough non-retirement-account cash set aside to cover the taxes for the conversion. And the tax on Roth IRA conversions can indeed be expensive. Let's say you have a $250,000 traditional IRA and you decide to convert all of it to a Roth IRA. You'll owe income taxes on $250,000, or about $87,500 in federal income tax (in addition to state income tax), assuming you're in the 35% tax bracket. On the plus side, the money you pay in conversion income taxes reduces your estate, which could minimize possible estate taxes.

There are a lot of variables to determine whether it makes sense to do a Roth IRA conversion, including whether income tax rates and your own tax bracket are likely to rise or fall after retirement, and if you have enough non-retirement-plan funds to cover the up-front tax hit. A Roth IRA, for example, might make sense if you have a large estate and expect to be paying income taxes at a higher rate in the future than you are now. You're also allowed to do partial conversions if you don't want to convert all of your money all at once.

One factor to consider, though, is your estate plan. Since, unlike regular IRAs, there are no minimum required distributions with a Roth, and your heirs won't owe income taxes when they take withdrawals, it could make sense to convert to a Roth for its estate-planning benefits. As I discussed earlier, after you pass away, your non-spouse Roth beneficiaries must take minimum distributions, but the money, while in the Roth, accrues tax-free, and distributions are still free of income taxes to your beneficiaries. That's a nice gift to leave for heirs.

## EMPLOYEE BENEFITS AND SOCIAL SECURITY

If you have an employer-sponsored retirement plan, such as a 401(k) or pension, you'll need to get in touch with your employer's plan administrator to get a beneficiary form and to determine whom you can designate as a beneficiary. Rules for employer-sponsored plans vary, depending on the plan. In general, you must name your surviving spouse as a primary beneficiary of an employee-sponsored plan, unless you get a waiver from your spouse. (Make sure to update your forms, however, if you get a divorce.)

What if you have clocked years on the job at the same company, earning plenty of back pay or vacation time, but die before receiving the benefits to which you're entitled? When you are no longer alive, your spouse may be eligible for such benefits as back pay or corporate life insurance. (Make sure, though, to designate heirs on your corporate life insurance beneficiary form.) A surviving spouse or other beneficiary should contact your employer to see if he or she might be eligible, as policies vary by company.

Meanwhile, what about Social Security? If your spouse

(and in some cases, your ex-spouse) was eligible for Social Security benefits, you may be able to receive survivor's benefits. Typically, for surviving spouses to receive at least partial Social Security benefits, they must be age 60 or older, or have children under age 16. If surviving spouses are disabled, they may be able to collect benefits even earlier. Surviving minor children, dependent parents and even ex-spouses married to the decedent for more than ten years or caring for the deceased's minor children may also be able to receive survivor's benefits. Contact the Social Security Administration (www.ssa.gov and type in "survivor's benefits") for more information about your situation.

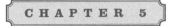

## CHAPTER 5

# TRUSTS

rusts were once thought of as a financial planning tool for the super-rich. But trusts can be a very important estate-planning tool even if you're not swimming in money.

While the word "trust" might evoke images of mind-bending financial complexity and Rockefeller-size bank accounts, in its simplest form a trust generally is nothing more than an agreement to hand over your assets to someone else—a "trustee"—who then minds those assets for your beneficiaries. When you set up and fund a trust, you are considered to be the "grantor," while those who benefit from the trust are called the "beneficiaries."

Depending on how they are structured, trusts can be used for a wide variety of things: for example, to avoid the difficulties and expense of probate proceedings; save on estate taxes; support a favored charity while providing an income stream to the benefactor; provide for children from a previous marriage—or even support your pet after you die. Trusts also are being used as financial tools beyond the realm of traditional estate planning. For instance, doctors, executives and other individuals concerned about being sued are increasingly using trusts to protect their assets from creditors.

The growth in trusts has partly been spurred by changes in the legal landscape. Lawyers are devising more-flexible versions—making it easier, for example, for beneficiaries to switch trustees or make other adjustments as tax laws or family situations change. There also have been overhauls in trust laws, which vary by state, including laws designed to make trust assets tougher for creditors to reach.

## TRUST BASICS

Trusts fall into several categories. They can be "irrevocable," which means you generally can't undo the trust after setting it up, or "revocable," which allows you to change the provisions at any time. They can also be "living" (otherwise known as "intervivos"), which means they go into effect while you are alive, and generally avoid probate. Or trusts can be "testamentary," which means they go into effect upon your death, as indicated by your will, which goes through probate.

As I discussed in the previous chapter, the most common type of trust is a revocable living trust, because these trusts are useful to keep certain assets out of probate—the legal process of administering an estate after someone dies—and to designate someone else to manage your property if you become incapacitated.

This chapter, however, focuses chiefly on irrevocable trusts, which provide a host of other benefits. The first is tax-related. Since you are irrevocably shifting assets out of your ownership, the tax man may not consider some of those assets part of your estate. So you might want to consider an irrevocable trust if you are worried that you might be hit with estate tax.

Another reason to set up an irrevocable trust: to protect family assets from the possibility of lawsuits, creditors or an

### A NOTE ON TRUST ASSETS AND DIVORCE

Depending on state law and how the trust is drafted, a trust left to a child may sometimes be *counted* as your child's asset during his or her divorce proceedings, when deciding which spouse gets what. However, trust assets are unlikely to be *distributed* to your child's ex.

ex-spouse who goes after the property. Rules vary, but the general idea is "if you don't own it, nobody can take it from you," Las Vegas estate lawyer Steven Oshins said.

## TRUST PITFALLS TO AVOID

Before setting up a trust, make sure to consider some caveats. Trusts can have setup costs of thousands of dollars, plus annual trust management and accounting fees that can eat away some 1% of trust assets annually. They also can be highly complex, with lots of legal jargon, acronyms and tax rules, so it is important that a reputable trust lawyer carefully walk you through what you are signing.

Unlike most investments, in which you regularly can track performance, you might not be around to see if your trust ends up working as intended, given that many trusts kick in only upon death. It is smart to sit down and discuss your trusts with your heirs, to help prevent any fractious family fights or litigation down the road.

And while many irrevocable trusts can save a bundle on estate and generation-skipping taxes, they aren't total tax shelters. The trusts themselves are typically subject to federal and state income taxes, and heirs usually must pay income taxes on their trust distributions. Meanwhile, revocable living trusts—the most popular type of trusts—don't provide any special tax advantages but have a number of other non-tax-related benefits, such as avoiding probate, as we talked about in the previous chapter.

Once you decide a trust is the right way to go, you don't want to do the planning on the fly. It is worthwhile to use a lawyer who is a trust and estate specialist, given that even a slight misstep in designing a trust could cause it to malfunction down the line or trigger unintended tax snafus. State laws governing trusts also vary dramatically, so make sure that your legal team is familiar with the laws where the trust and trustee are located, as well as where you and your beneficiaries live.

## A TAXING MATTER: GRANTOR TRUSTS

Trust creators can structure a trust as a "grantor trust." That means that you can set up a trust so that you—the grantor—pay the income taxes on the trust's earnings, rather than having the money for taxes come from the trust itself.

If you pay the income taxes on the trust's earnings, you're effectively leaving more money for your heirs, because it allows more of the trust assets to go to your loved ones rather than to the IRS.

## NAMING A TRUSTEE

Choosing the right trustee, and the right mechanism for naming successor trustees over time, is a key decision for anyone creating a trust. It has only grown more important as more families create long-term trusts to last for many generations, or even forever.

Typically, people name family members, dependable advisers or financial services firms to serve as trustees. Responsibilities include investing and monitoring the trust's money, ensuring that tax forms and other paperwork are filed and making payouts to beneficiaries.

There are lots of factors to consider when deciding whether to name a relative, a close friend or a financial institution as a trustee. If you decide to use a relative or friend, it can be tough to find suitable replacements for them when they die or in the event that they become incapacitated. It may also be hard to find qualified individual trustees if you are setting up a trust in a faraway state that has trust-friendly laws, as it's advisable that the trustee live in the state where you are setting up the trust.

On the other hand, large financial services firms may provide impersonalized service, suffer from high staff turnover and impose hefty trust management fees—and may also try to push their own investment products on trust clients. However, even though bank trustees may lack the personal touch of Uncle Harry, they may be more impartial than family members, and come without the emotional ties that can become problems when family members manage a trust.

When weighing whom to name as a trustee, consider the following questions:

- Does the trustee understand my family history?

- Does the trustee have a solid track record managing investments?

- How much does the trustee charge?

- Has the trustee ever been sued in a trust or investment-related lawsuit?

- Is the trustee located in a state with trust-friendly laws?

Bank trustees typically charge around 1% of trust assets to manage the funds (although the fee percentage usually decreases the larger the trust fund). That said, if you choose to use a bank or trust company, it is worth trying to negotiate this expense, particularly if you have a long-standing relationship with the financial institution or you have a multimillion-dollar trust fund.

Contrary to popular belief, choosing an individual trustee isn't necessarily cheaper than choosing a financial services company, though. Many states set fees for trustees that are applicable even if your trustee is Uncle Harry, though these can be waived if everyone agrees.

Some families opt to have it both ways and use co-trustees, typically a family member and an institutional trustee, who share responsibilities and serve as checks and balances. (When designating co-trustees, you should include a mechanism, such as requiring a mediator or arbitrator, for resolving disputes if they arise.) Some trust creators even designate what are known as "trust protectors," who generally have the power to fire and hire trustees.

Regardless of whom you choose to serve as trustee, make sure to include a clause in your trust allowing you or your heirs to switch trustees if necessary. Changing trustees can still be a hassle in some states and may involve a trip to the courthouse, but it's much less of a pain than staying with a bad trustee.

# TRUST TIP SHEET

Irrevocable trusts come in a wide variety of flavors and can be used for many purposes. In this section, I'll go over some of the most widely used types of irrevocable trusts, including trusts for minor children, trusts to benefit spouses and various tax-saving trusts. (I'll talk about some other important types of trusts throughout the book. For discussions of irrevocable life insurance trusts, see Chapter Six; charitable trusts, see Chapter Seven; special-needs trusts, Chapter Eight; and pet trusts, Chapter Eight. I also discussed revocable living trusts in Chapter Four.)

## TRUSTS FOR YOUR CHILDREN

One of the most popular reasons to create a trust is to leave money to minor children. Children under the age of 18 can't inherit directly more than just a token amount of money. Without advance planning, if you and your spouse pass away, a court will appoint a property guardian—who could be a complete stranger—to handle your child's inherited assets until he or she reaches adulthood (either 18 or 21, depending on state law).

There are several steps parents can take to prevent that situation. (I'll talk about naming guardians for your child's care later on, in Chapter Eight.) Perhaps the simplest way is to set up a custodial account for your kids in your will. In this instance, you name a custodian who will decide how the money should be managed. The catch is that once your children legally become adults, they will inherit that money outright. That's fine if your kids are the responsible types, but it's not so good if they are bad with money. (Also note that if you name yourself as the custodian of your kids' accounts, the money will be counted as part of your estate, so it's smart to name someone else as the account custodian if you're worried you'll have a taxable estate.)

An alternative to a custodial account, then, is to set up a trust for your minor children—often called a "minor's trust"—which gives you a bit more control over what happens to the assets even after you are gone. The trust funds can be used to support your children while they are still minors, according to directions you set out for the trustee. But unlike with a simple custodial account, once your children reach adulthood, they don't automatically have to receive the money outright.

There are several different ways you can set up a trust for your children. You can set up a testamentary trust so that it goes into effect only upon your death, if you pass away while your kids are still minors. Or you can set up an intervivos trust to support your kids or grandkids even while you are living. For instance, many parents or grandparents set up educational trusts, which hold funds to support a loved one's college, graduate school or private school education. Some parents or grandparents choose to make annual gifts to such a trust while they are still alive.

Trusts can be set up with a wide range of provisions, depending on the values that are important to you and your family's situation. For instance, some people include special provisions, called "incentive provisions," which can reward heirs with distributions for good behavior, such as finishing college, or punish them by withholding distributions for poor behavior, such as drug use. (I'll discuss incentive provisions in more detail further on.) Some trusts include "spendthrift clauses," which restrict an irresponsible beneficiary from

## PROTECTING SPENDTHRIFT CHILDREN

Some parents are concerned about leaving large inheritances for their children because they are worried they might spend the money too quickly or rashly.

One solution is to leave money for your heirs in a trust, rather than outright, but give the trustee clear directions on how and when—and when not—to distribute money to beneficiaries. (For instance, a spendthrift clause could cut off distributions if an heir has a drug or gambling problem.)

In addition, or as an alternative, to using spendthrift trusts, you can mandate in your will that your executor buy an annuity from an insurance company to fund your heir's inheritance. An annuity typically pays monthly income and can prevent your heir from burning through the cash all at once. (I'll discuss annuities in more depth in Chapter Six.) While this strategy is smart if your heir has problems managing money, it is not recommended if your heir has a substance abuse problem, because an annuity provides a regular flow of cash.

squandering the trust's principal on gambling, drugs, alcohol or other reckless behavior. You can set aside money for private school or college funds, or you can restrict spending to basic support, such as food, education and health care. The trustee you name has the responsibility to make or withhold distributions based on the provisions that you include in the trust. The trust's provisions, though, should be flexible enough to allow some leeway as your child's needs change.

You can also specify or delay the age when the money is distributed to your kids, or parcel out the money in chunks over time, so your kids don't inherit it all at once when they're, say, 18, and perhaps not the best money managers. Traditionally, many parents created trusts that paid out when the kids reached specific ages—some disbursements when a child reached 25 years old, then more at 30, then 35—after which point, the trusts dissolved. But in recent years, more lawyers have been advising parents to leave gifts or inheritances, even

## INCENTIVE PROVISIONS

When you set up a trust, you can put in what are known as "incentive provisions." This means that you attach certain strings to the trust in order to pass along your values. A trust might say, for instance, that heirs only get their shares if they finish college, or that beneficiaries might be disinherited if they abuse drugs or alcohol.

Be very careful, however, when setting up incentive provisions because you risk ruling your heirs with a dead hand. Also, some stipulations can backfire. For instance, some trusts have provisions matching distributions with the amount of income a beneficiary earns. While the idea might be to discourage laziness in future beneficiaries, in reality you might just end up penalizing a child who chooses a noble but low-paying profession, such as social work or teaching, or chooses to stay home to raise a family, in favor of an heir who makes big bucks.

Also, avoid including incentives or restrictions in a trust that violate public policy. A clause stipulating, for instance, that your heir cannot marry someone of a certain race or religion might not pass muster.

small ones, in longer-term trusts. The idea is that money left in trust for as long as possible is safer—from creditors, divorcing spouses and estate taxes—than money given outright. A trustee would have the discretion to give money to your kids as needed, as set out in the trust documents.

## TRUSTS TO RECEIVE YOUR OWN INHERITANCE: INHERITOR'S TRUSTS

As I discussed earlier, many estate planners say a smart way to leave your heirs money is in a trust, rather than outright. That's because money received in a trust, if structured properly, can be protected from your heirs' creditors or in a divorce, and in some cases may be passed on to the heir's own children free of estate taxes.

I've just gone through how to plan ahead for your kids'

inheritances. But what about any money you expect to receive from your own parents or relatives?

If your parents already left you a windfall outright, your options are limited. But if your parents are alive, estate planners are increasingly recommending that you discuss with them the possibility of amending their own estate plans to leave any inheritance to a custom-designed trust—an inheritor's trust—which is essentially like an empty box to hold whatever assets are left to the trust.

Just as you can create trusts for your own kids, your parents can create inheritor's trusts for you in a variety of ways. However, there are a few rules to maximize the tax and asset protection benefits. First, the trust must be set up before you actually receive the inheritance. Second, you shouldn't fund it yourself for your own benefit. In most cases, these trusts are used for inheritances or gifts from parents, but they also can be funded by other people, such as grandparents or close friends. Parents also can start funding the trust while they are still alive, rather than at their death.

Bringing up the topic of inheritance with parents often is the toughest part of the process. "It's hard for clients to go back to their parents and meddle into their affairs," said New York lawyer Gideon Rothschild. Some lawyers even have clients role-play the conversation, with the lawyers playing the role of the parents and clients bringing up the topic.

## Trusts for Spouses: Credit Shelter Trusts

In recent years, some of the most common types of irrevocable trusts were those designed for married couples to maximize their individual estate tax exemptions. Married couples, as you know, can pass on their wealth to each other estate-tax free. But when the surviving spouse dies, estate tax comes due. Until recently, without advanced planning, the couple could not always take advantage of both individual's estate-tax exemptions.

Here's where a special trust came in, often called either a "credit shelter" trust or a "bypass" trust. A typical credit shelter trust calls for the amount of the current maximum estate-tax exemption—$5 million in 2011—to go into the trust upon the first spouse's death. The surviving spouse would get distributions from the trust during her lifetime, and upon her death the rest of the trust's assets would ultimately go to the kids or other heirs, depending on the trust's instructions.

Upon the surviving spouse's death, the couple's kids would inherit money left over in the trust plus up to $5 million in the surviving spouse's estate, free of all estate tax.

Now, under the new tax laws, portability means that if you're married, your unused estate-tax exemption can be passed onto your spouse after your death. (I discussed portability in Chapter Two.) So, given portability, why still bother with a credit shelter trust?

Estate planners say there are several reasons why this vehicle is still useful, especially for couples with assets that are likely to exceed either the federal or state estate tax exemptions.

First of all, a credit shelter trust shields any appreciation of the assets placed in the trust from estate tax. So let's say you put in shares of stock worth $5 million into the trust and they rise significantly in value. All that appreciation is now out of your estate. (The downside, though, is that the assets left in the trust won't get a step-up in basis upon your death, which could mean greater capital gains taxes for your heirs. If the assets were left directly to your spouse, they would be stepped up to full market value upon your death.)

Leaving money in a credit shelter trust, rather than outright to your spouse or other heirs, can also protect assets from creditors. In addition, if your spouse remarries after your death, a credit shelter trust can help ensure that the remaining money goes to your kids, rather than to your spouse's new family. A credit shelter trust may also shield assets from being counted against Medicaid if your surviving spouse needs to go into a nursing home. Credit shelter trusts can be used to shield generation-skipping taxes, which are *not* portable. You can do this by making grandchildren beneficiaries of the trust and applying your GST exemption. And they can be used to protect both spouses' *state* estate tax exemptions, which, unlike the federal estate tax exemption, are not portable, at least as of this writing.

If you already have a credit shelter or bypass trust in your plan, talk to your lawyer about whether it's still appropriate for you, given the tax law changes.

Beware, though, that credit shelter trusts can become problematic as the estate tax exemption changes, as it did in recent years. The catch is that if your estate's total is right around the amount of the estate tax exemption, virtually all of your estate might end up in the credit shelter trust, leaving your surviving spouse with little to live on except for the trust's distributions. (You can lay out guidelines in your trust documents for how trust distributions should be calculated annually, or give your trustee discretion to handle distributions as needed.) Estate planners suggest that older couples, especially, revisit their estate plans regularly to adjust the amount intended for the credit shelter trust if necessary.

You and your spouse may also need to retitle your assets in order to properly fund your credit shelter trusts. Let's say you have $7 million in your own name, and your spouse only has $500,000 in her name. While you would be able to fund a $5 million credit shelter trust, your spouse couldn't. Note that you can't transfer ownership of your retirement accounts while you're still living. That can make things tough if one spouse has a very hefty IRA (enough to fund a credit shelter trust) while the other spouse has peanuts.

What about jointly owned property? If a husband and wife own property jointly with rights of survivorship, the assets pass directly to the surviving spouse upon the first spouse's death. Thus, these assets can't really be shielded in a credit shelter trust, because they go automatically to the surviving spouse, rather than to the trust upon death.

Review how your assets are currently titled and talk to your lawyer and financial adviser about whether you may need to shift ownership. (As I discussed in Chapter Three, rules are different if you live in a community property state.) You may also need to rebalance ownership every few years, just as you would your stock portfolio, if the value of one spouse's assets, say, goes south with economic and stock market shifts.

Another option is to leave money directly to your surviving spouse, but set up a credit shelter trust just in case. Your surviving spouse can disclaim, or give up, the money inherited directly and pass it on to the credit shelter trust if it seems like the right thing to do at the time. Disclaiming gives the surviving spouse discretion to decide how much money he or she needs at the time. As I discussed in Chapter Three, however, disclaiming an inheritance is full of complicated rules, so be very careful if choosing this option.

## Trusts for Spouses: QTIP Trusts

Nope, these have nothing to do with cotton swabs. Qualified terminal interest property trusts, or QTIP trusts for short, help prevent your money from going to a place where you may not want it to go—say, your wife's new husband and stepkids—after you die.

The trusts allow you to leave your surviving spouse with money from the trust to spend for the remainder of his or her lifetime, but upon your spouse's death, the leftover QTIP trust assets pass as *you* indicate in the trust, rather than how your surviving spouse chooses. Many blended families use QTIP trusts to ensure that children from a previous marriage get any remaining assets from the trust once your spouse is gone.

Although QTIP and credit shelter trusts sound similar,

## POWERS OF APPOINTMENT

When you create a trust, you can name whomever you would like as beneficiaries. When you die, however, those beneficiaries become set in stone—unless you hand someone else the power to change beneficiaries, which is called a "power of appointment."

These powers come in two flavors: "limited powers of appointment" and "general powers of appointment." The limited power is when you give someone (your surviving wife, for example) the power to change beneficiaries among a limited group of people, such as your children, but *can't* give the property to herself, her estate or her creditors. This limited power can be useful if you want to leave property to your kids but don't want to set in stone that they will each receive assets in equal shares. Giving your surviving spouse a limited power of appointment can allow her to, say, reward a particularly helpful child or provide less to a bad seed.

If you give your wife a general power of appointment, however, she has the power to switch beneficiaries completely after you are gone, transferring property to the beneficiaries of her choice or even to herself. In short, you should only give a general power of appointment to someone who understands your wishes and whom you completely trust. Otherwise, your property could end up with someone you may not particularly want as a beneficiary. For that reason, general powers of appointment are not used very often.

they have different tax treatment. If you create a QTIP trust that benefits your surviving spouse, no estate taxes are due upon your death. But, because of tricky tax laws, when your spouse dies, whatever's left in the trust will be included in your surviving spouse's estate, and may be subject to estate taxes if the estate is big enough. In essence, for large estates, a QTIP trust defers estate taxes, rather than eliminates them, but gives the trust creator more control over where the money ultimately ends up.

Some very wealthy families, therefore, use QTIP trusts in combination with credit shelter trusts. They place the maximum amount that can be sheltered from the estate taxes in credit shelter trusts, and stick some of the money left over in QTIP trusts to ensure more control after death.

## TRUSTS FOR REAL ESTATE: QPRT

Homes are the most valuable asset in many estates. A qualified personal residence trust, or QPRT (pronounced "Q-pert"), allows families to pass on the future appreciation of a house's value to heirs, free of estate tax.

This tactic is great if you expect your house to appreciate in worth, as real estate did for many years, since you're essentially removing that appreciation from your estate. However, there may be a gift tax when using a QPRT, because you are essentially making a discounted gift of your house to your kids.

Here's how a QPRT works. You (a parent) transfer the deed of your house into a trust and are entitled to live in that house for the length of the trust, which can vary. (In this example, let's say the trust is designed to last ten years.) When you set up the trust, your house was worth $1 million, but ten years later your house is now worth a whopping $6 million. When the ten-year trust ends, the house, regardless of its appreciated value, passes to your two children and out of your estate, free of estate taxes.

Do you owe any gift tax if you set up a QPRT? The answer, as with many things tax-related, is that it depends. With QPRTs, special IRS formulas determine the value of the gift to your children, based on several factors: what your house was worth when it was placed in the trust, the length of the trust, and a special interest rate set by the government each month, which I'll discuss in more detail further on. According to tricky tax laws and actuarial calculations, the longer the length of the trust and the higher the interest rate, the smaller the potential gift tax bite.

But beware: if you, the parent, die before the trust ends, the property goes right back into your estate—valued at the time of your death. So the strategy works best if you expect to live for at least another decade or so. And even if you outlive the trust, note that your heirs could face considerable capital gains taxes if they eventually sell the house, because with a QPRT, your heirs don't get a step-up in cost basis when the trust term ends. (I discussed the concept of step-up in cost basis in Chapter Two.) Also, make sure to consult with your lawyer before setting these up, because there are lots of tricky tax rules to consider.

What if you outlive the length of the trust and don't want to move out of your home? You can continue to live in the house by paying your kids rent at fair market value. While having your kids serve as your landlord may be disconcerting, it's actually another way to transfer more wealth to them without incurring any estate tax.

## TRUSTS FOR APPRECIATED ASSETS: GRATs

There are other trusts that, like the QPRT, help remove assets from your estate sooner rather than later, to avoid taxes on future appreciation. Let's say you bought shares of a promising stock at virtually nothing. The idea is to get those shares out of your estate early, so if they balloon in worth, that appreciated value is not subject to estate taxes.

One way to do this is a "grantor-retained annuity trust," or GRAT. These trusts, whose life span can be as short as two years, are popular with families who have assets that are expected to increase in value, such as depressed stock or shares in a private company that eventually goes public. If the assets perform well, much of the appreciation in the trust can pass to heirs tax-free when the trust ends.

In a typical GRAT, a parent transfers assets to a trust and receives fixed annuity payments from the trust for a set period of time. A GRAT is subject to a special interest rate, set by the government. (I discuss this more in the box on page 91.)

## INTEREST RATES AND TRUSTS

Many trusts are required by tax law to use a special interest rate, issued by the Internal Revenue Service each month. A number of popular trusts, such as grantor-retained annuity trusts (GRATs), qualified personal residence trusts (QPRTs) and charitable trusts, are sensitive to interest rates, and their success changes when rates climb or fall.

The rate is basically how much the IRS estimates a trust will earn for tax purposes, regardless of how much its assets actually appreciate over time. It is essentially an assumed rate of return. The rate, known as the "7520 rate" or "hurdle rate," is linked to Treasury bond yields and is used to determine the possible tax bill when setting up a trust.

Certain strategies, such as GRATs and charitable lead annuity trusts (CLATs, discussed in Chapter Seven), work better when rates are low, while other tactics, such as QPRTs and charitable remainder annuity trusts (CRATs, discussed in Chapter Seven), work better in a higher-interest-rate environment.

When considering a trust strategy, make sure to discuss with your lawyer and accountant current interest rates and whether rates are projected to move higher or lower in the future. Waiting a month or two to take advantage of a higher or lower rate could make a real difference down the line.

This interest rate is locked in when the trust is created. With a GRAT, the lower the rate, the greater the chances of passing more money to beneficiaries.

If structured properly, the parent will end up getting back the principal he or she placed in the trust, plus the interest set by the rate. Whatever the trust earns above the rate, however, goes to the children, tax-free, when the trust ends.

One big caveat: if you die during the trust's term, trust assets could be taxed as part of your estate, defeating the trust's purpose.

Still, advisers say that the trusts have little downside or tax risk, though setup fees can range from $2,000 to more than

$10,000. And because they are short-term, often lasting just a couple of years, you're not tying up your money for long if circumstances change dramatically.

## WHERE TO LOCATE YOUR TRUST

Your irrevocable trust is a separate entity and doesn't have to be located in the state where you live. In fact, some states, such as Delaware, South Dakota, Alaska, Nevada, Florida, Wyoming and New Hampshire, have passed new laws that make these places particularly attractive for setting up a trust.

Such "jurisdiction-shopping" to find attractive trust laws has grown more common, and some individuals are even moving existing trusts to different states to take advantage of better laws.

Going out of state for a trust may not always make financial sense, especially for smaller trust accounts, and it can come with a number of hassles. It's also not applicable for revocable living trusts, since they don't have any special tax benefits.

First of all, to set up a trust outside your home state, you generally need to use a trustee located in that state, typically a trust company, lawyer or family member or friend who lives there. Since the most favorable jurisdictions might be in states where you don't know an individual trustee, you might need to hire an institutional trustee, which will charge a commission for managing the assets. Plus, moving an existing trust may also involve hefty lawyers' fees of at least several thousand dollars and may require court approval, depending on how the trust was originally drafted and state law. And though improvements in technology have made people more comfortable with banking remotely, it can still be a hassle to deal with a distant trustee.

So why go outside your own state? With trust laws literally all over the map, here are some factors to consider when seeking a home for your irrevocable trust funds:

**Avoid state income taxes.** Trust experts say one of the first factors to look for when examining where to set up a trust is whether the assets are subject to state taxes. The idea is to let trust investments grow for as long as possible free of state taxes, which can save significant sums of money, especially in high-tax states such as New York and California. (Beneficiaries, however, may be taxed on distributions, depending on whether their home state has an income tax.) Alaska, Florida, Nevada, South Dakota, Texas, Washington and Wyoming, for instance, are attractive because they don't impose any state income taxes on personal trust assets.

Each state has its own tricky tax rules for trusts. For instance, Delaware and New Hampshire generally don't impose a tax on trust assets if the beneficiaries live out of state. And California might try to tax an out-of-state trust if one of the beneficiaries lives in California. The situation can get even more complicated if you use co-trustees located in different states, or if there is real estate in the trust. Make sure to check with lawyers familiar with laws in the state where you live and where your trust is located.

**Seek flexibility.** Trusts are typically drafted to have two sets of beneficiaries—current and future. Current recipients, often a surviving spouse, traditionally receive income distributions. Future beneficiaries, often children or grandchildren, eventually receive the trust principal, the actual assets placed in trust. In the past, that has led to fights between beneficiaries over how the trust funds should be invested. A surviving wife, for example, might want the trust assets to be invested primarily in safe, income-producing bonds or dividend-paying stocks to maximize her income, while the children might prefer a more aggressive portfolio to boost principal.

To prevent those conflicts, more than forty states and jurisdictions have a "power to adjust," which gives trustees flexibility to make distributions, even if that means tapping a trust's principal. And many states, including Delaware,

Alaska, California, Florida, Illinois and Pennsylvania, have "total-return unitrust" statutes allowing trusts to pay current beneficiaries a fixed percentage of trust assets—often between 3% and 5%—rather than simply paying out the income generated by the trust. Laws allowing for such distribution options can help prevent battles among beneficiaries down the road.

**Keep wealth in the family with a dynasty trust.** Another factor to look for in comparing state laws is how long a trust can last. In recent years, a number of states have undone a centuries-old law called the "rule against perpetuities" that placed time limits on trusts, often about 90 to 120 years. Now, more states are allowing "dynasty trusts" that can last for hundreds of years or even forever. One attraction is that, if structured properly, money inside the trust can pass through many generations without incurring additional estate or generation-skipping taxes, allowing the trusts to build large gains over time. More than twenty states and jurisdictions, including Delaware, New Jersey, Wisconsin, New Hampshire, Illinois and Virginia, now allow such long-lasting trusts.

In a typical dynasty trust, a grandparent transfers assets to the trust, below the amount of the estate, gift and generation-skipping tax exemptions (so it's not subject to those taxes upon your death). The trust holds and invests the money for beneficiaries—the children, grandchildren, great-grandchildren and beyond. As long as the money stays in the trust, it can pass from generation to generation without additional estate or generation-skipping taxes, so the trust accumulates vast sums over time. After a hundred years, a dynasty trust funded with $1 million could grow to $867.7 million, assuming a 7% annual growth rate, according to an analysis by Wilmington Trust.

There are many ways to fund a dynasty trust, including using life insurance or by selling interests in a business to the trust. One of the simplest ways is to make annual exclusion gifts to the trust ($13,000 is the current gift tax exclusion) so the money isn't subject to gift taxes. The money in the trust will appreciate during the rest of your lifetime and will be out of your estate. You can then leave more money to the trust at death. Any further appreciation in the trust after your death should be free of additional transfer taxes, if structured properly.

There are some downsides, however, to trusts that last for the long haul. Dynasty trusts can demotivate children or grandchildren to work, since they know that they'll receive regular trust income. Also, as the number of beneficiaries grows over time, there's more of a chance for family disputes. And although dynasty trusts save a bundle on estate and generation-skipping taxes, they also can incur perpetual annual fees and expenses that can cut into a trust's value over time.

Still, dynasty trusts can ensure that family wealth doesn't dissipate in a generation. One woman I interviewed set up a dynasty trust in South Dakota several years ago to help pass the family's primary asset—commercial real estate—to her two children, six grandchildren and beyond. This trust, valued in the "high eight figures," should accumulate significantly over the years, said the woman, a Nevada resident. "The trust is effectively keeping the assets that you have worked very hard to assemble from being confiscated in a couple of generations," she said.

**Protect your assets.** Doctors, business executives and other professionals have been increasingly interested in asset protection trusts. With these, you transfer your money into a trust run by an independent trustee, who has discretion over the money but can give you distributions when needed. These trusts, if set up properly, are supposed to be out of reach of creditors in legal judgments.

In the past, individuals concerned with liability flocked to create trusts in offshore locales, such as the Cook Islands and Nevis. Now, a growing number of states, including Alaska, Delaware, Rhode Island, Nevada and South Dakota, permit these trusts. However, asset protection trusts set up in the United States haven't been adequately tested in court, and it's unclear how well they will hold up, experts say.

## A DEEPER LOOK
# ASSET PROTECTION STRATEGIES

Asset protection, or placing your money where it's safe from lawsuits or creditors, was once considered a shady practice. Now it's moving into the mainstream.

People who are vulnerable to a lawsuit, bankruptcy or divorce—and it's a surprisingly big group, including doctors, corporate executives, business owners, real estate investors and even families with teenage drivers—have grown increasingly concerned about protecting their property.

The goal of any plan like this is simple: to create as many hurdles as possible for potential creditors to jump through. Most plans are also designed to encourage your creditors to make a favorable settlement with you, rather than face long and perhaps expensive litigation.

One big caveat: if you know you have a potential legal action looming, don't transfer a big chunk of assets out of your hands. It's too late, because courts are likely to rule it a "fraudulent transfer." Also, the federal bankruptcy law enacted in 2005 changed the asset protection landscape, making it tougher in some instances to protect your home from creditors.

The good news: it isn't necessary to shell out tens of thousands of dollars to set up a complex offshore trust or partnership. Some effective and perfectly legitimate asset protection strategies can be both simple and cheap, such as putting more money into a 401(k) plan, which is off-limits to most creditors under federal law.

A person at risk of liability could also transfer money to his or her spouse's name, but beware: if your marriage breaks up, so will this strategy.

There are scores of questionable asset protection "experts" who are hawking their tactics in seminars, online and in kits. It can be tough to detect them, but there are a couple of warning signs. Be careful if you're required to sign a non-disclosure form, since if something is done legally, you should be able to show it to your estate-planning advisers. Be wary if the plan seems too complicated. And make sure to work with a lawyer who is well versed in your own state's laws.

Here is a breakdown of the strategies that advisers are now recommending:

- **Segregate business and personal risks.** Place businesses, including family businesses, inside a corporate shell such as a limited liability company or a family limited partnership. If creditors go after your company because of a business problem, they will have a hard time taking any personal assets.

- **Buy "umbrella insurance."** One of the first lines of defense is to shift your risks to another entity, such as an insurance company. Umbrella insurance protects assets from personal injury claims above the liability limits set by standard-issue home or auto policies.

- **Maximize state exemptions.** The laws governing protection of assets such as homes and insurance policies vary by state. In Florida and Texas, you can transfer your wealth into your home (building an addition, say, or paying off a mortgage), life insurance policy, annuity or retirement plan, all of which are generally exempt from creditors. In some states, married couples can title their property jointly in a special way called "tenancy by the entirety," which can make it tough to reach if a creditor goes after one spouse. In tenancy by the entirety, which isn't available everywhere, each spouse owns the entire, undivided property, rather than a share of the property, as in traditional joint ownership. Therefore, neither spouse can sell or transfer the property independently of the other. In practical terms, this form of ownership means that a creditor of one spouse can't go after the property unless the creditor has judgments against *both* spouses together. More details about your state's laws are available at www.creditorexemption.com.

- **Use trusts.** Doctors, executives and other professionals are increasingly turning to asset protection trusts, in which you transfer a portion of your own money into a trust run by an independent trustee, who controls the money but can give you occasional distributions. If set up properly, these trusts are supposed to be out of reach of creditors.

  As I mentioned earlier, the trusts have long been created in offshore jurisdictions, such as the Cook Islands and Nevis. The idea is to put money in a foreign place that doesn't recognize a U.S. court order. In recent years, a growing number of people are setting up asset-protection trusts in the United States, as several states, including Alaska, Delaware, Rhode Island, Nevada and South Dakota, have started permitting them over the past decade. You don't have to be a resident of one of these states to set up a trust there.

  Offshore trusts generally cost at least $25,000 to set up; domestic asset protection trusts generally can cost less than half of that. But remember, domestic trusts haven't been adequately tested in court, and it's unclear whether they will be upheld.

- **"Equity-strip" your assets.** That's a fancy term for loading your property with debt so that it's less attractive to creditors. Let's say you have a vacation home you want to safeguard. Take out a bank loan against the value of the property and place the loan proceeds into an asset, such as an insurance policy or annuity, if such assets are exempt from creditors in your state.

The theory: if the house is loaded with debt, it isn't going to be attractive to another creditor. The downside: you'll have to come up with a way to pay back the loan.

## CHAPTER 6

# LIFE INSURANCE

Life insurance is one of those financial products that can give people the heebie-jeebies. It can sound confusing and complicated (term? cash value? whole? universal? variable?), and like other aspects of estate planning, it involves thinking about a very scary proposition: death.

But life insurance really isn't as frightening or complex as it seems. It's actually a fantastically useful and flexible estate-planning tool that can provide income-tax-free security for your loved ones. If you set up a special trust, life insurance proceeds can be free not only of income tax but also of estate tax. And life insurance proceeds typically avoid probate, because you name your beneficiaries directly in the policy, rather than in your will.

Life insurance can provide income and living expenses for your spouse, children or other loved ones after your death. It can support your favorite charities. It can also provide liquidity to pay off estate taxes—especially if your estate largely consists of illiquid assets such as real estate, fine art or collectibles, or a closely held business that you may be reluctant to sell to raise cash. Life insurance can help heirs retain a beloved family vacation home or help maintain a family business. And it can be used to pay off any debts your estate might owe, such as bank loans.

There are also numerous ways to use life insurance to help a charity. For instance, depending on state law, you might name a charity as a beneficiary of your policy or use a policy to back up a pledge, in case you die before you are able to fulfill the obligation.

For starters, though, let's look at how you go about getting insured and the basic types of life insurance.

## LIFE INSURANCE 101

To get a life insurance policy, you can go directly to an insurance company or use a broker, who compares products from multiple insurance companies and can help you find the best quote. Online brokers, such as www.accuquote.com, www.insurance.com, www.insure.com, www.quickquote.com and www.term4sale.com, can help you compare and find good deals on policies, too. You can also check if your company, union or trade association offers a group life insurance policy. Group life insurance policies may not offer as much flexibility as some individual policies, but they typically don't require a medical exam—a boon for those in poorer health seeking to be insured.

When you're shopping for policies, stick to companies with high financial strength ratings from firms such as A. M. Best Co., since the last thing you want when spending money for peace of mind is to have to worry about your insurer going bust.

Most individual life insurance policies require you to get a medical evaluation so that the insurer can assess your health and longevity risks. That's typically arranged by your insurance broker or the insurer, at no cost to you. In most cases, a medical technician will come to your home or office to get some vital stats and blood and urine samples.

Usually life insurance premiums become more expensive as you get older and your health declines. So, as I mentioned, if you're in poor health, consider a group insurance plan, which may be available through your employer, union or trade association, and which covers a large number of people of varying health. These plans typically don't require a medical exam. You might even be able to convert it to an individual policy when leaving your job, for a fee.

How do you know whether you should get life insurance? You generally can skip life insurance if you're single with no dependent kids and don't expect to have a taxable or debt-ridden estate. Also think twice about forking over for life insurance if your premature death wouldn't affect the ability of your surviving partner to pay for day-to-day living expenses.

But do consider life insurance if you have dependent children or if your spouse doesn't work or you have a big income disparity. In these cases, if you die prematurely, a life insurance policy can help the survivor pay for your family's day-to-day cost of living, including mortgage payments.

There are many variables to factor in when considering how much life insurance to buy. It depends on your current and projected income and assets, your family's annual living expenses, the length of your policy, and whether you have any specific future economic needs, such as a child's college tuition, a special-needs child who needs lifelong support, or expected estate taxes to pay off. Your insurance broker or salesperson can help you come out with a coverage amount that's suitable for your situation.

## TERM LIFE

Life insurance, in its most basic form, can be divided into two categories: term and permanent or cash-value. "Term life," the simplest and cheapest form of life insurance, is when you buy an insurance policy that lasts for a set term, typically ten, twenty or thirty years.

The product, which usually costs just a few hundred dollars a year if you're in good health, is appropriate for people who only want life insurance for a limited amount of years—such as until your children are grown or until you reach retirement age.

My husband and I, for instance, bought a cheap ten-year term policy when we were expecting our first child. We did it to provide peace of mind that our family would be provided for in case either my husband or I pass away when we're in our prime income-producing years. As the ten-year-term draws closer to an end, we may consider renewing the policy, depending on our health and the cost, or we may switch to permanent coverage, which would last for the remainder of our lives.

Many term life insurance policies these days have level premiums, meaning that you pay the same amount annually to keep your coverage.

## Permanent or Cash-Value Life Insurance

This is insurance that lasts for the remainder of your lifetime, rather than for a set term of, say, twenty years. "Permanent policies," also called "cash-value policies," are often used for specific estate-planning purposes, such as funding future estate taxes or for ensuring the continuity of a family business.

These plans are more costly than term life insurance because they last longer and because they provide more than just a death benefit: they also have an investment component in which money accumulates tax-free within the policy. In other words, a portion of your premium is placed in a separate investment account; this money grows tax-free while the policy is in force. (How it's invested depends on the policy.) As more money builds up inside the policy, you can eventually use this stash of cash to help you pay the policy's premiums, or you can borrow against the policy if you need some extra cash flow.

Many insurers tout the tax-free investment benefits of cash-value policies. Not only does the money grow inside the policy tax-free but you can also withdraw your premiums without a tax penalty. What's more, your beneficiaries don't have to pay income taxes when they receive the policy's payout.

That's in contrast to a traditional individual retirement account, in which your heirs eventually have to pay income taxes on the IRA's distributions. A cash-value policy might also make sense, say financial advisers, if you have already contributed the maximum amount to other tax-deferred investment accounts, such as 401(k)s and IRAs.

On the other hand, the higher premiums, high commissions, and sometimes limited investment choices might not make a cash-value account worth it. My husband and I decided, for now, to follow the maxim "Buy term and invest the difference." In other words, we bought a cheap term policy rather than an expensive cash-value plan and are investing the difference in our 401(k)s, IRAs and other funds.

If you already have a term policy but a permanent policy sounds more attractive, don't fret. Many insurers give holders of term policies the right to convert to cash-value plans without a new medical exam. That means your premiums for the converted term-to-permanent policy may be less expensive than if you were to buy a brand-new permanent plan.

There are three main types of cash-value plans. "Whole life" offers fixed (but usually not astronomical) bond-like returns, with a guaranteed minimum return. "Universal life," like whole life, typically has a low guaranteed minimum return but offers more flexibility in adjusting the size of the premiums and the death benefit during the course of the policy. Universal life is also usually invested in funds that earn interest at varying rates, so as interest rates rise or fall, you either can earn more or less.

"Variable life," meanwhile, lets you choose from a wide range of investment options, from money-market funds to foreign stocks, which means higher risk but potentially greater reward over the long term. Variable life typically has no minimum guaranteed return, though. (There is also a version of variable life for very high net worth investors called "private placement" life insurance, which allows you to invest in hedge funds, with tax-free profits, within your insurance policy.)

Some people choose to buy a special kind of permanent policy called a "second-to-die" or "survivorship" policy. These policies pay out when the second person in a couple—you or your spouse—dies, and the money generally goes to your children or other heirs. They typically cost less than traditional permanent insurance because they are based on the life expectancies of two people, rather than one.

Survivorship policies can be useful to cover situations when one spouse is healthy but the other spouse is in worse condition and has trouble obtaining insurance on his or her own. They can also be used for estate planning. Married couples typically don't owe estate taxes upon the first spouse's death. However, they may owe taxes when the surviving spouse dies. A second-to-die policy can be used to cover estate taxes in those situations.

## POLICY OWNERSHIP AND LIFE INSURANCE TRUSTS

Typically, most people own insurance policies on their own lives or on their spouse's lives. Owning a policy yourself means you have total control over the policy. You can change beneficiaries or cancel it at any time. But the problem with such ownership is the death benefit is considered part of your estate when you die.

So for estate-tax purposes, some wealthy families use other forms of policy ownership. One tactic is to have your children be the owner and beneficiary of a policy on your life. That strategy can be successful if your chief goal is to pass on your wealth to them. What's more, since the policy is owned by your kids, not by you, it is considered out of your estate.

But by giving up direct ownership, you technically give up certain rights, such as the ability to change beneficiaries. And take note that if your children receive the death benefit outright, that can be a problem if a child is young, has trouble with responsible money management or owes creditors. Also, you may have to make outright gifts of cash to your kids so that they can afford to purchase the premiums on the policy.

As an alternative, many wealthy individuals turn to another way to buy life insurance: an "irrevocable life insurance trust," or ILIT. Such trusts can shield big life insurance policies from estate taxes as well as income taxes.

When you set up an irrevocable life insurance trust, the trust, rather than you or a family member, owns the insurance policy, pays the premiums and receives the death benefit when you die. Since the trust isn't owned by you, it is considered out of your estate and not subject to estate tax. You cannot be the trustee, but your spouse can, as long as the trust is drafted and managed carefully. Money from the trust can then be distributed to your beneficiaries, such as your children.

The trust can buy a new life insurance policy outright on your life. Or if you have an existing insurance policy but worry that your estate may eventually be subject to estate taxes, you can transfer the existing policy to a trust. However, such transfers can be subject to gift taxes and run another risk. According to tax rules, you must live for three years after setting up an ILIT or after transferring an existing policy to an ILIT, or the policy will be counted as part of your estate—and, if large enough, possibly subject to estate taxes. (The IRS requires this to prevent last-minute deathbed policy transfers.)

What about changing beneficiaries? If you are the policy owner and are of sound mind, you have complete freedom to change beneficiaries. But you must do so directly on the insurance policy by filling out the appropriate paperwork through your insurer, rather than through your will or trust. If you transfer ownership to a trust or to your children, you lose direct control over beneficiary designations.

## CRUMMEY POWERS

In order for a life insurance trust to own an insurance policy, the trust itself needs to pay the premiums on the policy. That means you must transfer money into the trust so that the trust can pay the insurance premiums. The problem is that such transfers from you to the trust, for various complex tax code reasons, may be subject to gift taxes if not made properly.

However, many life insurance trusts use what are called "Crummey powers," named after a party in a decades-old tax-related court case. Crummey powers can allow you to avoid or minimize taxes when transferring money to an insurance trust. Crummey powers are complicated and involve a bit of pesky paperwork, so make sure to get good legal guidance and be very careful in executing them.

In order for such Crummey gifts to be tax-free, you can transfer up to $13,000 each year, per beneficiary, to the trust (the current gift tax exclusion in 2011). Now, here's where the extra work kicks in: you have to tell the trust's beneficiaries, *in writing,* that you have made a gift to the trust, and give the beneficiaries a window of opportunity of at least thirty days, every year that the trust is in force, to withdraw the money if they so choose. Your hope is that your heirs will choose not to take the money now but instead will let the trustee use the money to buy insurance premiums.

Notifying beneficiaries about such gifts may seem like a lot of extra red tape, but tax experts recommend doing this in order for the gifts to pass muster with the IRS.

## ANNUITIES

How can annuities, a popular retirement-planning tool, be used for estate planning? Annuities, in their most basic form, provide a steady stream of income during retirement. In short, you give an insurance company a lump sum of money in exchange for regular payments for the rest of your life or for a certain period of years. The annuity's payments are either a fixed or variable amount, depending on the type you choose.

Traditionally, annuities didn't offer a lot of estate-planning options. With old annuity products, when you died, the insurance company typically kept whatever money was left in the contract. So if you bought a $500,000 policy one day and then tragically passed away the next day, the insurer, rather than your estate, might have kept the $500,000.

Now, however, you can add options to annuities that allow you to leave part of the annuity to your heirs, although sometimes in exchange for a lower regular payout. For instance, you can name another person as a successor beneficiary to the annuity contract after you are gone. Or you can buy a "joint and last survivor" annuity, which continues to pay out as long as either you or your spouse is still alive. Or you can guarantee that your kids will receive part of the annuity's remaining principal if you die before a certain time. Make sure to weigh whether the cost of any extra riders is worth the benefit, especially if you already have life insurance to provide adequate financial protection for your spouse or other heirs.

Also beware that your heirs may owe income taxes on some types of annuities, depending on the contract. While annuities are tax-deferred for you (the owner), your heirs may not be so lucky. Instead, because of tricky tax rules, heirs to annuities may end up with substantial income tax hits. And if you own the annuity directly, it may end up as part of your estate.

The bottom line: make sure to carefully research the income tax and estate tax consequences of an annuity before buying one. Annuities are complicated, come in lots of varieties and are often peddled by aggressive salespeople who glide over the negative tax and estate-planning consequences.

## LIFE SETTLEMENTS

In life, of course, your financial needs change. You may receive a windfall, such as an unexpected inheritance or a lottery jackpot. Your children or spouse may pass away. A child might make it big and no longer need your support financially. What happens if your financial circumstances change and you don't need your life insurance anymore?

Most people simply stop paying their premiums, termi-
nate their insurance coverage and receive whatever cash value
has accumulated in their policy. But in recent years, a new
option, called a "life settlement," has emerged. That's when
you sell your insurance policy to someone else, who, in effect,
cashes in when you die.

In a life settlement, you sell investors the right to death
benefits from your life insurance policies. The buyer, typically
an institutional investor, takes over the premiums for your policy and reaps the payout when you die. In exchange, you get
cash while you are still alive.

Life settlements sound creepy. After all, a stranger is essentially profiting from your death. But the transactions have
a number of benefits. By selling to a third party, you can get
much more than what you would receive from your insurers by surrendering the policy. For instance, if an insurance
company is willing to pay $50,000 to buy back a policy with a
$1 million death benefit, a life settlement company might pay
$200,000.

These transactions can also be attractive for policyhold-
ers who might not have the means to pay future premiums
nor the desire to do so if, for example, all their beneficiaries
have passed away. Selling an insurance policy frees up cash
for current needs, such as pricey long-term care, especially if
the policyholder doesn't have other assets that can be easily
liquidated.

Selling a life insurance policy is also an option if you find
yourself needing cash quickly. Such was the case for one man
I interviewed when he went over budget on a new house he
was building. So the man, a mortgage banker from Annapo-
lis, Maryland, started shopping two policies, with a combined
death benefit of $2 million, that he had taken out on his el-
derly mother.

He had been paying $35,000 a year in premiums for the
policies, he said, but the insurer would have paid him virtually
nothing to cash them out. So instead he fielded bids through

a life settlement broker. A small firm offered $205,000. He accepted.

"I didn't really look at it as morbid," said the mortgage banker, who had been supporting his mother financially. "I thought, 'Wow what an incredible way to put a value on this.' " His mother had been in poor health but approved of the sale—she was fine with him seeing the money now rather than later, he said.

Beware, though, of tax consequences; if you sell a policy, you generally owe taxes on the money you receive in a life settlement.

And, of course, if you sell your policy to a third party for a quick cash infusion, your heirs, if you have any, might be up in arms that a stranger will be receiving the policy's death benefit instead of them.

## INSURANCE, TAX AND SUCCESSION STRATEGIES FOR FAMILY BUSINESSES

Owners of a family business sometimes use life insurance to help ensure the continuity of their companies. Life insurance proceeds help businesses weather the rough months after a key employee or owner dies—or can help provide liquidity to the business owner's family, whose assets might be tied up in shares of the business they can't or don't wish to sell.

It's common, for instance, for business owners to have what's called "key person" insurance. That's when the business itself buys insurance on the life of the owner, with the policy's proceeds paid to the business or to the owner's heirs, especially if it's a family business.

Another business strategy is setting up a "buy-sell" agreement, which is a formal contract that obligates a partner to sell to or buy out another in the event of death, disability or another catastrophic event. Typically, these agreements set a sale price for your share of the business. Life insurance is a common way of funding such an agreement. Partners take out policies on each other and use the death benefit to purchase the other partner's business share.

And here's a tax deferral strategy for family businesses: For most taxable estates, taxes are due within nine months after death (or fifteen months with an extension). But if you have a closely held businesses that makes up more than 35% of the value of the gross estate, under Section 6166 of the tax code, you may be able to make estate tax payments in up to ten equal annual installments—and the first payment isn't due until five years after the original due date. Thus you may be able to stretch out your payments for many years. A downside is that the IRS charges interest on these deferred payments, so your business must be able to cover those costs. Check with your estate lawyer to see if your closely held business qualifies for this tax treatment.

What about passing on business interests to your heirs? Family business owners must think especially carefully about how they want to bequeath shares of the business to their children, especially if some kids work in the business and others do not.

For instance, if your daughter worked diligently in the business for years, helping to make a division profitable, while your son chose a different pathway, you might want to leave a controlling interest of the business to your daughter, while leaving your son with assets comparable in value, such as life insurance or a house.

If you have a family business, I recommend consulting with a lawyer or other adviser familiar with business succession planning. (You can find advisers who are experts in family business succession through the Family Firm Institute, www.ffi.org.) I also recommend that you start early when thinking about and communicating your succession plans with your family.

One man I interviewed said his family decided to get extra help to figure out their succession plans. The man is the fourth generation of an Oregon family that operates

beverage distribution companies and forest products businesses. His generation was starting to get more involved in
the business, and the family wanted to make sure it carefully
communicated its business succession and estate plans early
on, to preempt future conflicts. Twice a year for several years,
the man attended three-day family meetings with his cousins,
parents, uncle and aunt. The meetings were facilitated by an
estate lawyer and a psychologist who worked with families on
communication.

"It's to ensure that our family will continue as a family,"
he told me.

At the meetings, family members gave presentations
about their businesses, so all attendees were up to speed about
the companies. The family also developed a family mission
and value statement and is working on a family constitution
that will outline how the business should be governed. "We
definitely have energetic and exciting conversations about
these types of things," he said.

## CHAPTER 7

# PHILANTHROPY

**M**any people want to bequeath part of their estates to support charities they believe in—leaving a legacy of helping out the less fortunate, nurturing the arts or supporting other important causes.

You also get some significant tax breaks when you leave money to charity. Because it's considered out of your estate, money left to charity is not subject to estate taxes. Charitable gifts are not subject to gift taxes, either. (In fact, gifts made while you're alive can even generate income tax deductions.) And donating, rather than selling, appreciated assets during your lifetime, such as shares that have gone way up in value, can help minimize capital gains hits. Furthermore, some charitable vehicles that I'll talk about in this chapter, such as gift annuities, can generate a nice income stream for you or your heirs. For many, the opportunity to benefit good causes while reducing taxes and sometimes even generating income is a perfect estate-planning solution.

Charities and non-profits, many of which have "planned giving" specialists on staff, are well aware of these tax benefits and are willing to work with you to maximize the impact of your donation on your estate, your family and the charities you wish to support.

Let's start our discussion of ways you can leave your money to charity with one of the most straightforward forms of philanthropy: a bequest.

## BEQUESTS

A "bequest" is a direct gift to a charity through a will. Money left to a tax-exempt charity (known in estate-planning parlance as a "501(c)(3)" entity) is considered out of your estate, so it's not subject to estate taxes, or gift taxes, either. Of course, because a bequest is made through a will and becomes effective after you die, you won't be able to enjoy an income tax deduction for the gift. Also, an individual can't make a direct charitable gift to another individual, such as to help an impoverished friend; such contributions would be considered gifts rather than charitable donations.

A famous example of a very large bequest is the $1.5 billion that Joan Kroc, the wife of McDonald's founder Ray Kroc, left to the Salvation Army in 2004. She also bequeathed $200 million to National Public Radio and smaller amounts to numerous other charities.

Although some bequests come as huge surprises to charities and the public, it's best to discuss your plans with the charity in advance, so it can be prepared for the money and make plans for how best to use it.

It's also smart to talk with your family members about your bequest, so they understand why the money is going to the charity and not to them.

When you make a bequest, you can attach strings, such as asking the charity to use the money to fund a certain cause. For instance, Kroc's gift to the Salvation Army was to be used for the development of community centers across the country that offered educational, recreational and cultural programs. Talking to the charity in advance about any restrictions to the donation can help prevent misunderstandings going forward.

Wills, of course, are revocable, so you can change a bequest at any time. Some people, upset with the direction or management of a charity, have changed charitable gifts in their wills. An elderly acquaintance of mine, for instance, had planned to leave a large collection of magic memorabilia to a museum. When he became miffed at the museum's board, he changed the terms of his bequest. He ended up selling off the collection during his lifetime, rather than leaving it to the museum.

## DONATING FROM YOUR IRA

For 2011, Congress has allowed another way to benefit charity: giving directly from your IRA. Under the new rules, individuals who are 70½ years old and older may directly transfer, tax-free, as much as $100,000 in 2011 from their IRAs to charity. The gifts count toward IRA holders' required minimum distributions, which would otherwise be taxed as income.

There are some caveats. Donors can't take a tax deduction for these donations, and the gifts have to be made directly from the IRA to charity. (You can't withdraw the money first and then donate it.) Also, some types of charities, such as donor-advised funds, charitable trusts and most private foundations (all of which I'll discuss in this chapter), can't be recipients of these transfers. In addition, you can't receive any goods or services in exchange for the gift. And whether the IRA gifts will be allowed after 2011 depends if Congress votes to extend the law.

Giving from an IRA might make sense for seniors with well-funded IRAs who already have plenty to live on, or for individuals whose required minimum distributions would bump them into a higher tax bracket. But before donating from an IRA, consider whether it might make more sense to give other appreciated assets during your lifetime (for which you can get an income tax deduction and reduce possible capital gains taxes) and bequeath assets in your IRA after death by naming a charity as one of your beneficiaries in your beneficiary-designation forms (thus saving your heirs income taxes on their distributions). Every individual's situation varies, of course.

# POPULAR CHARITABLE-GIVING VEHICLES

If you are positive that you want to donate some of your estate to charity, you may want to consider an irrevocable gift, which you can make during your lifetime, through a charitable trust, gift annuity or foundation. These gifts, if made while you're alive (rather than through a will, as in a bequest) have many benefits: they can earn a nice income tax deduction while you're still around to use it, they move money out of your estate so there's less money subject to potential estate taxes and they help out a good cause.

Some irrevocable vehicles, such as a charitable lead or remainder trust, or a charitable gift annuity, can also provide funds for family members.

Many large charities, as mentioned earlier, have planned giving departments or staffers who can help you set up these trusts or other giving structures, but it's smart to have your own counsel to make sure the terms are beneficial to both the charity and your family. Here's how some common charitable vehicles work.

## CHARITABLE REMAINDER TRUSTS

With these popular charitable trusts, you transfer assets to an irrevocable trust, which then pays you or your family income for a set period of time, or until you or your heirs die. At the end of the trust's term, whatever money is left in the trust goes to a charity designated by you, the donor.

Charitable remainder trusts typically come in two flavors, called "annuity trusts" and "unitrusts." In an annuity trust, you or your family will receive a fixed annual gift from the trust, typically based upon your life expectancy. In a unitrust, the income stream fluctuates annually, because it's based upon a percentage of the trust's value each year. A charitable remainder trust of either type must pay out a minimum of 5% each year, and the charity must receive at the end of the term at least 10% of the original gift, according to IRS rules.

The donor receives an up-front tax deduction for the money expected to be received by the charity at the end of the trust's term, based on calculations set out by the IRS. The income stream that you or your heirs receive, on the other hand, is taxable.

Many people donate appreciated assets, such as stock that has risen in value, to charitable remainder trusts. The advantage is that by donating the shares to the trust, the trust can sell the shares without being subject to capital gains taxes, and then can use the cash to benefit both the charity and you (although, as said above, you'll owe some income tax on the payments you receive).

The money inside the trust is typically invested by the trustee in conservative investments. Even if the trust investment has poor returns, the donor is typically entitled to the distribution amount specified in the trust documents. The trustee of a charitable trust is often the charity itself, but it could be you or your family or a financial institution or adviser, too.

How do you know what amount to take for the up-front tax deduction? As in all things tax-related, the answer is tricky. Each month, the IRS sets a special interest rate (officially called a "7520 rate," but often called a "hurdle rate" by estate planners) to estimate how much of the money in the trust will pass to the charity at the end of its term. When the rate is higher—it changes each month, so check with your accountant or lawyer—the IRS assumes the trust will earn more, and more money will end up with the charity at the end. That means a bigger tax deduction for donors.

## CHARITABLE LEAD TRUSTS

Charitable lead trusts essentially operate in the reverse manner as charitable remainder trusts. In a charitable lead trust, assets are donated to an irrevocable trust that then pays a stream of income to a designated charity. At the end of the trust's term, whatever money is left in the trust goes to your heirs. You can create a charitable lead trust either during your lifetime or upon your death, through your will.

Charitable lead trusts, like remainder trusts, come in two varieties. In a charitable lead "annuity trust," the income stream received by the charity is fixed when the trust is set up. In a charitable lead "unitrust," the charity receives a percentage of the trust's value each year, so the income stream will fluctuate based on the trust's investment performance.

Note that gifts to charitable lead trusts, like charitable remainder trusts, are irrevocable, so once you put assets in, you generally can't take them out. And if the trust's value goes down over a period of time, your heirs could receive less, because the trust will make its charitable payments regardless of market conditions, meaning the depreciation will eat into your heirs' piece of the pie.

The taxation of charitable lead trusts can be complex. Donors can choose to take an up-front income tax deduction based on the trust's expected income payments to the charity. However, many donors choose to forgo that tax break because of complicated IRS rules surrounding the deduction.

Like a charitable remainder trust, the IRS each month sets a special interest rate, dubbed the "hurdle rate," to estimate how much of the money in the trust will pass to your heirs at the end of the trust's term. Unlike charitable remainder trusts, charitable lead trusts are usually more attractive when hurdle rates are low, because any appreciation in the trust above the hurdle rate goes to your heirs, tax-free, when the trust is over.

It's important to note that the money that ends up with your heirs at the end of the trust's term may also be subject to gift taxes. However, charitable lead trusts may be structured in such a way to avoid or minimize gift tax consequences. This strategy is called "zeroing out" the trust, which means that the income stream to the charity equals the amount of the principal originally transferred to the trust. (If structured properly, your heirs may get the extra amount that the trust earns free of any gift tax.) Your estate lawyer and your designated charity can help you set up a zeroed-out trust.

## CHARITABLE GIFT ANNUITIES

Charitable gift annuities work a lot like charitable remainder trusts, except they are simpler and usually less expensive to set up.

Legally, charitable gift annuities are considered contracts rather than trusts. You can set them up directly with a charity, usually without having to pay the sometimes hefty legal fees needed to set up an individual charitable trust. Indeed, setting up a charitable trust may involve several thousand dollars in lawyers' fees, depending on how complicated the trust's terms are.

With a charitable gift annuity, you give a sum of money directly to a charity, rather than to a trust, which promises to pay you a fixed amount regularly for life. (The amount is based, in part, on your life expectancy.) Although a portion of the annuity payments is taxable, you'll also receive an up-front income tax deduction for the amount estimated to end up with the charity upon your death, based on IRS calculations.

For more information on charitable gift annuities, you can check out the website of the American Council on Gift Annuities (www.acga-web.org).

# PRIVATE FOUNDATIONS

Many wealthy families think about creating private foundations either during their lifetimes or upon their death. For some families, it's the ultimate status symbol: a charity that's under a family's complete control and that can, through strategic gifts, have a major impact on the cause or issue they care most about. (Famous examples include the Gates, MacArthur and Rockefeller foundations.)

When you are setting up a private foundation, you're, in essence, setting up your own tax-exempt charity. But instead of soliciting donations from the general public, like so-called public charities such as the March of Dimes or the Red Cross, a private foundation's funds typically come from a single individual, family or corporation, rather than the greater population.

A private foundation makes grants each year to support a charitable mission. The IRS requires private foundations to distribute at least 5% of their investment assets each year for charitable purposes. (Many charities, though, distribute far more each year, or try to invest the remaining funds in low-risk vehicles to build an endowment for the long haul.)

The appeal of a private foundation for donors is control. The donor has total say over the decisions the foundation makes, including where grants are made and how foundation money is invested (subject to IRS rules against "self-dealing," such as using the foundation's money to enrich the donor's family).

Private foundations can also have estate-planning bene- fits. Money contributed to the foundation, either during your lifetime or upon your death, is considered out of your estate for tax purposes. What's more, private foundations can be a great way to get other family members, such as your children or grandchildren, involved in your family's charitable endeav- ors, sometimes for many generations.

The downside of a private foundation is that it can cost several thousand dollars in legal and accounting fees to set up, plus a good deal of money, time and paperwork to manage over the long haul. And if you want the private foundation to continue after your death, you need to set up a management plan to ensure that it's in good hands when you are no longer around.

In addition, the IRS offers less generous income tax benefits to donors to private foundations than those to public charities. For instance, if you donate cash to a private foundation, you typically can deduct only up to 30% of your adjusted gross income (AGI). Contributions to a public charity, by contrast, can be deducted up to 50% of AGI.

## DONOR-ADVISED FUNDS

In recent years, a growing number of families have turned to an alternative to private foundations called "donor-advised funds." In a donor-advised fund, an individual typically contributes cash, stock or other assets to the fund, gets an immediate income tax deduction for the contribution, and recommends how the money should then be distributed to charitable organizations.

In other words, the fund legally controls the money, but the donor recommends how it is distributed and to which charities. The donor can postpone for years the task of choosing which charities to support, while selecting investments from a menu that may include mutual funds or other options.

The funds, which are considered public charities, are offered by charities affiliated with major financial institutions such as Fidelity Investments and Vanguard Group, as well as community foundations and other groups. Funds often require minimum initial gifts ranging from $5,000 to $25,000 and charge fees of roughly 1% for administering and investing the money.

Donor-advised funds are popular because they require less paperwork and offer better income tax breaks than starting a private family foundation. Additionally, donors can make one contribution and let the donor-advised fund handle sending the checks to a bunch of separate charities. Reporting donations for tax purposes is easier with a donor-advised fund than when giving directly to a lot of charities, which could mean sorting through a year's worth of charitable receipts.

When one woman I interviewed began contributing to a donor-advised fund set up by her local community foundation, the vehicle's simplicity was a big selling point. While "there's a good bit of work" involved in starting a private foundation, "somebody else is doing the work here for us," she said. She has used the fund to make grants to local organizations, including a gift to the local YMCA.

Donor-advised funds, which are run by public charities, also offer more generous income tax treatment than private foundations. Individuals can deduct up to 50% of adjusted gross income (AGI) for donations of cash, compared to just 30% of AGI for gifts of cash to private foundations.

And of course, like all charitable gifts, money given to a donor-advised fund is considered out of your estate for tax purposes.

Both private foundations and donor-advised funds can offer an easy way for your heirs to continue your philanthropic legacy after you pass away. These vehicles are thereby good for those who aren't quite sure what causes they'll later want their money to support. Unlike a typical bequest, in which you have to designate specific charities in your will, if you leave money to your private foundation or donor-advised fund, your heirs can choose recipient charities down the road, based on your guidance or wishes.

Some donor-advised funds, such as the Fidelity Charitable Gift Fund, allow you to name successors to continue to advise the fund on distributions after your death or incapacity. And some funds have endowment programs, in which the fund continues to make regular grants to charities that you designate for a set period after you die. Or you can request that a certain favored charity receive a lump-sum distribution upon your death. Policies vary, so check with the donor-advised fund of your choice to see what its rules are.

# DONATING ASSETS OTHER THAN CASH

Giving to charity doesn't just mean donating cash or writing a check. Many people choose to give appreciated stock, real estate, land, tangible assets (such as art, collectibles or used cars) or even intangible assets (such as patents). Some people, for instance, have arranged to donate their homes to charity, or have arranged for so-called conservation easements on their property, which can help preserve the land from future development while providing a tax break.

Some donors have approached charities with gifts bordering on the bizarre. The National Philanthropic Trust, in Jenkintown, Pennsylvania, for example, has received inquiries about gifts ranging from a surfboard collection and an antique army tank to a chain of adult bookstores. The Community Foundation for the Fox Valley Region, in Appleton, Wisconsin, received a doll collection valued at several hundred thousand dollars. Other charities have accepted a vineyard, a share in a car dealership, a dozen or so technology patents and a membership in a fancy golf club.

An advantage of donating appreciated assets, rather than selling them, is that you can avoid paying capital gains taxes when you make a donation. That's particularly helpful for gifts of art and collectibles, which in 2011 had maximum capital gains rates of 28%, rather than the 15% rate for appreciated securities.

Beware, though, that the IRS has a number of complicated rules for donations of non-cash assets, such as collectibles, cars and real estate—and the rules vary, depending on what sort of asset is donated. For one, under the tricky "related-use" rule, the size of the deduction can depend on how the charity you pick will use it. That means that donors get a bigger deduction if the charity can actually use the object—say, hang it on a museum wall—rather than quickly sell it off for cash. So talk to your estate-planning lawyer or accountant to make sure you understand the tax treatment of your donation.

Also make sure that the charity accepts gifts of non-cash assets, such as securities, real estate or personal property. Not all charities have the means to handle such gifts, so before unloading your great-aunt's watercolor paintings on your favorite charity, make sure that it can actually accept the gift.

And if the object is likely to be worth more than $5,000, you should make sure it gets independently appraised, in writing, at the time it is given. Appraisal costs vary widely depending on the asset but usually run several hundred dollars. Keep written records of the property's appraisal, as well as all receipts from the charity.

## EVALUATING CHARITIES

Once you've decided that you want to donate some of your estate to charity, the next part is deciding where to give and what vehicle you should use to make your contribution. But, really, how hard can it be to give money away?

Pretty tough, actually, since these days, donors have thousands of charities to choose from, not to mention many financial instruments with which to give away their dollars. If you're feeling overwhelmed, philanthropy advisers—ranging from free online services to paid consultants—can help donors identify causes, vet charities and measure donors' bang for the buck.

Several websites evaluate charities or provide detailed information on charities' operations. Charity Navigator (www .charitynavigator.org) rates charities on their financial health and efficiency, and the American Institute of Philanthropy (www.charitywatch.org) gives charities letter grades based on criteria such as how much the charity spends to raise $100.

Several sites don't give grades but provide valuable information about charities' operations. The Better Business Bureau's Wise Giving Alliance (www.give.org) issues reports on

## PAYING SOMEONE TO HELP
## GIVE AWAY YOUR MONEY

Wealthy donors and private foundations—typically those who give upward of half a million dollars—are increasingly turning to philanthropy consultants to provide due diligence, for a fee, on the charities they already support or are considering funding, sometimes using deeper data than that provided by simple IRS filings.

For instance, Geneva Global (www.genevaglobal.com), a for-profit group that focuses on philanthropy in developing countries, says it would assess HIV counseling and testing programs by measuring the percentage of individuals who consent to be tested and the total cost per patient, among other metrics. Other donor advisers include the non-profit Rockefeller Philanthropy Advisers (www.rockpa.org) and the Philanthropy Initiative (www.tpi.org), also a nonprofit.

The cost of hiring an adviser varies. Some firms charge about $500 to $3,000 a day, while others charge a percentage of charitable grants, typically from 3% to 15%.

Several professional organizations can direct you to advisers, including the National Network of Consultants to Grantmakers (www.nncg.org) and the International Association of Advisors in Philanthropy (www.advisorsinphilanthropy.org). Community foundations, typically set up to help local causes, may be able to provide advice and research. For listings, visit www.communityfoundations.net or www.cof.org. The Council on Foundations (www.cof.org), Association of Small Foundations (www.smallfoundations.org) and National Center for Family Philanthropy (www.ncfp.org) also maintain lists of consultants and provide donor-education programs.

When vetting advisers, ask whether they are getting paid by any organization they recommend for funding. And request references from former clients.

One man I interviewed, a trustee of his family foundation, hired Rockefeller Philanthropy Advisers to help the foundation identify recipients for the $1 million it hoped to grant annually to environmental health programs. The foundation's trustees had tried to research projects but found it too time-consuming. The consultancy invited environmental health experts to speak at a daylong event in New York, helping the foundation pinpoint recipients.

charities and determines whether they meet some twenty financial and governance standards. There is also www.guidestar.org, which provides a database with information, such as tax forms, on more than a million non-profits.

Charity watchdog groups offer a guiding principle in evaluating charities: if a charity doesn't answer your questions about its operations or finances or provide Internal Revenue Service filings or annual reports, think twice about giving. Also look carefully at a charity's overhead: generally less than 40% of your donation should be spent on administration and fund-raising, according to the American Institute of Philanthropy.

All of the free evaluators rely to some extent on IRS Form 990, which must be filed by many charities. (In general, faith-based groups are exempt.) The catch is that the information charities provide on the form often is incomplete or inconsistent, making it tough to glean accurate financial information about a charity solely from that paperwork, or to compare groups with each other based on it. Also, the form doesn't give any information on how effective a charity is at actually fulfilling its mission, such as how well it provides the homeless with job training, for example.

That means you need to do a little more legwork on your own, beyond the free evaluators, to find out which organization you want to put your money behind. Donors should ask non-profits about their goals and strategies, and about which indicators they use to monitor their own impact. You should see how the charity measures its results both in the short term—monthly or quarterly—and over a period of years. Check the charity's website or annual report for specific details on how it gauges its results. If the information isn't there, call the charity and ask.

Another great way to get to know a charity: volunteer with the group to experience its work firsthand, or visit a site to get to know staffers, clients and facilities.

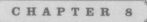

## CHAPTER 8

# PREPARING FOR THE UNTHINKABLE

In previous chapters, I talked about how to plan for your money and other assets after you're no longer here to watch out for them.

In this chapter, however, I'll discuss perhaps a more crucial issue: making plans to take care of your loved ones—and even yourself—when you're no longer able to do so. Measures you'll need to take include creating power-of-attorney documents for finances and health care if you become incapacitated, and naming guardians for your children if you are no longer able to take care of them. I'll also cover how to provide long-term security for family members with special needs, and how to ensure your pets will be cared and provided for when you are unable to do so.

This important component—planning ahead in the event of your own incapacity—is too often overlooked. An AARP study of 1,500 adults age 45 and older found that only 39% had a power of attorney for health care decisions, while just 27% had created a financial power-of-attorney document.

This chapter will help demystify this piece of estate planning, starting with setting up a power of attorney.

## POWER OF ATTORNEY FOR FINANCES

A "financial power of attorney" is a legal document that authorizes an agent—usually a spouse, another family member or a trusted adviser—to make financial decisions if you become unable to make them yourself.

The point of setting up a power of attorney is to name an agent while you're still in good health and can make clear decisions. Obviously, it's important to designate someone trustworthy, since the agent has wide latitude over your finances. Because a power-of-attorney arrangement is a private agreement between you and your agent, there is no court supervision.

Make sure to carefully lay out exactly what powers you want your agent to have. For instance, you can limit the agent's power to make gifts of your property, so the agent can't just give money to himself (though hopefully the person you choose wouldn't consider doing this). Spell out under what conditions gifts can be made, how much and to whom.

There are two main kinds of power-of-attorney documents. If you're using a "springing" power-of-attorney document, which goes into effect only when you are declared incapacitated, make sure to carefully specify how you are to be deemed incapacitated. You can ask, for instance, that your agent get a second medical opinion to make sure you really are unable to handle your own affairs.

A durable, "non-springing" power-of-attorney document, meanwhile, goes into effect immediately upon signing. ("Durable" is a legal term that means the power of attorney will continue to be effective if you become incapacitated.) That can be useful in a case where an agent wants to immediately take control to stop, say, abuse by a neighbor or caregiver, without waiting for a doctor's declaration of incapacity. However, you really need to trust your agent if you're going to do a non-springing power of attorney.

Other lawyers suggest using a non-springing document but not handing it over to your designated agent. Instead, tell the agent where it is, and once you become incapacitated, he or she, can retrieve it.

A power of attorney ends at your death, when your agent can no longer continue to act on your behalf.

Lawyers say that powers of attorney are often a tough balancing act: you want them to be simple for trusted family members or friends to implement, so they don't have to jump through too many hoops each time they need to, say, pay a necessary bill or deposit a check. But you also want to avoid giving agents a license to steal or use your money against your wishes.

To further protect yourself, you can require that your agent provide family members, or a third party, such as a lawyer or accountant, with regular accounting statements. Another strategy is to name co-agents. While that can be a pain for them—many financial transactions, for instance, would need two signatures—it can also create a system of checks and balances. In some cases, lawyers appoint an additional safeguard: a "protector," who has the power to replace the agent if there is wrongdoing. Talking through your needs and concerns with your lawyer is the best way to determine the arrangement best suited to your situation.

In the unfortunate event that your agent is accused of financial impropriety, there is some recourse. Another loved one can petition a court to name a protective guardian or conservator, as I'll discuss in more detail in this chapter. Typically, court-appointed guardians can be another family member or a third party, such as a lawyer, a bank, a social worker or a specially trained professional guardian. If you yourself sense wrongdoing, you can contact your local district attorney's office, many of which have elder-abuse units, and let them investigate.

Power-of-attorney laws differ from state to state, so make sure your lawyer is familiar with what your state allows. Rules also can vary by financial institution. Lawyers say banks are

## JOINT-CHECKING ACCOUNTS

Seniors can use another simple solution for financial management in the event they are incapacitated: setting up a joint checking account in both their name and their adult child's name. This allows adult children to sign checks to pay parents' bills when necessary. Parents can set up such arrangements account by account, adding a child's name to a checking account, for instance, but still retain control of a savings or brokerage account.

Estate planners still recommend that seniors have powers-of-attorney documents in case they become more incapacitated, and to handle assets that aren't covered by a joint-checking arrangement. In addition, joint accounts can have tax and other downsides, which I discussed in Chapter Four. For instance, your co-owner could potentially withdraw all of the assets in the account without asking you first. You need to really trust your child or other joint-account holder to have this arrangement.

increasingly scrutinizing power-of-attorney documents or are reluctant to honor them because they fear being subject to suits alleging they unwittingly helped an account be drained by an improper agent.

In addition, you can name an agent to be a "representative payee" to receive your pension, Social Security or other government income so that your agent can use that income to help pay your bills or other living expenses, if you're unable to do so yourself. To arrange this, contact your pension provider or the appropriate government agency for an application form and instructions.

Another option, in addition to the financial power of attorney, is to use a revocable living trust, which I discussed previously in Chapter Four. These trusts go into effect while you're still alive, and you can name another person as trustee to manage property in the trust once you become incapacitated. Many people name institutions, such as banks or trust companies, as trustees, if they're worried a family member might loot their money.

The trustee of a revocable living trust, however, only has control over the assets that have been transferred to the trust; by contrast, when you give someone power of attorney, he or she can manage assets that you didn't transfer to the trust. So even if you have a living trust, you should still set up power-of-attorney documents to handle assets not in the trust.

## GUARDIANSHIP: WHY YOU SHOULD PLAN AHEAD

If you don't name someone to have power of attorney for your finances and health (which I'll discuss later), a court might make the decision for you in a procedure called "guardianship" or "conservatorship."

Being under guardianship is more restrictive than having someone serve as your agent. Often, guardianship not only limits your right to make financial or health care decisions but also potentially keeps you from voting, marrying or entering contracts. In many cases, "you are reduced to the legal status of an infant," said Sally Hurme, a lawyer with AARP, the senior advocacy group.

Because guardianship is so restrictive, it's viewed as a last resort. Guardianship proceedings typically take place when an adult fails to plan ahead and designate who would handle his or her finances or health care decisions if he or she became incapacitated, so a court must name someone to take on those responsibilities. Guardianship proceedings can also happen if someone accuses a caregiver of neglect or financial impropriety and petitions the court to name a protective guardian.

If family members are feuding fiercely and if you haven't designated someone ahead of time to serve as an agent or guardian, a court might name a third party, such as a lawyer, a social worker or a specially trained professional guardian, to step in. Professional guardian fees must be approved by the court but are generally about $45 to $100 an hour, which is typically paid out of the incapacitated person's estate.

## AVOIDING GUARDIANSHIP: TIPS FOR PLANNING AHEAD

Here are some steps you can take ahead of time to minimize the chances of guardianship and other fractious court proceedings if you become incapacitated.

- Safeguard your power-of-attorney document by requiring that your agent provide family members or a third party with regular accounting statements. You can also name co-agents or limit the agent's power to make gifts of your property.

- If using a springing power-of-attorney document, which goes into effect only when you are declared incapacitated, carefully specify how you are to be deemed incapacitated. You can require, for instance, that your agent get a second opinion.

- Create a living trust. Many people have these in addition to power-of-attorney documents. You can transfer your assets into the trust and designate a trustee to manage trust property if you become incapacitated.

- Consider a clause in advance planning documents requesting that future feuds be settled with a mediator, which can be less adversarial and expensive than litigation.

- Talk about your wishes with your agents or trustees, as well as other family members and heirs.

- For more information on advanced planning, see the websites of AARP at www.aarp.org, the American Bar Association Commission on Law and Aging at www.abanet.org/aging, or the National Academy of Elder Law Attorneys at www.naela.org.

The bottom line: it's best to designate someone ahead of time as an agent for your finances and your health care. In your estate-planning documents, you can also specifically name someone as a guardian, if you ever need one, rather than have the court name someone for you.

## CHOOSING A GUARDIAN FOR YOUR CHILDREN

One of the toughest but most important estate-planning tasks is selecting a guardian for your children. Yes, you're choosing the person to handle the responsibility of raising your child if you and your spouse die or become severely incapacitated before your kids reach adulthood.

Selecting a guardian can lead to all kinds of family tensions. Some family members might be offended if they're not chosen, while others may not have the means or inclination to take on such an immense task.

You need not name a family member to take on the duty of guardianship, if doing so is not the best option in your particular situation. The most important criteria are that the guardian is responsible, has values you agree with, has the means to handle an addition to his or her family and will care for and treat your child in the way that you would wish your child to be cared for and treated.

Geography can also play a role; you might want to name someone who lives close to where your child already resides, or who lives close to other family members so there is a built-in support system.

If your child has special needs, your guardian should have a familiarity with your child's disability; in many cases, special-needs guardians serve in the role even when your child is older than 18. (See "A Deeper Look" on special-needs planning in this chapter for more information.)

You can name two separate people to serve as guardians— a "guardian of the person" takes care of raising your child, and a "guardian of the estate" handles your child's finances and inheritance. Although naming two guardians can serve as a system of checks and balances and can help prevent misappropriation of funds, it can also be a logistical pain for both guardians, who might have to check with each other and sign off to make decisions for your child.

In my family, my husband and I took the simpler route

and chose one guardian, my brother, to take care of raising our son and handle his finances. It was a tough decision, because my husband's brother and my sister also would have been very capable of serving as guardians. In the end, we chose my brother because he already had several kids, lives very comfortably and is geographically close to other family members who could help out raising our son if necessary.

It's definitely best to discuss guardianship with family members before writing it into your estate plan; that way, the role isn't just sprung upon them in the sad event their services are needed, and family questions (or resentments) about it can be aired and addressed earlier rather than later. You should also be sure to name a successor guardian in case the chosen guardian is unable to take on the role.

Guardianship decisions can be changed at any time, as long as you still have capacity; you should review your guardianship decision every few years to make sure that the person or couple you chose is still appropriate.

## A DEEPER LOOK
## PLANNING FOR FAMILY MEMBERS WITH SPECIAL NEEDS

Gabe is no ordinary trust-fund kid: he has epilepsy and Asperger's syndrome, a form of autism, which means that even though he is in his 30s, he still largely relies on his parents to provide for him financially. So his mother, Shelby Valentine, set up what's known as a special-needs trust, which will provide funding to pay for some of her son's expenses when Valentine and her husband are no longer able to care for him.

"It gives him a better quality of life after we are gone," said Valentine.

Parents of children with special needs often face years of medical bills and other expensive care, even once their kids reach adulthood. Now a growing number of financial services companies, lawyers and financial planners—often calling themselves "special-needs planners"—have emerged to help parents provide for kids with disabilities, especially when parents are no longer alive to provide care. These professionals guide families through the intricate maze of federal and state programs for disabled individuals and help set up trusts, insurance policies, retirement plans and estate-planning documents.

Experts often recommend that families create a "special-needs" or "supplemental-needs" trust as the centerpiece of their plan. Such trusts will provide funds to pay for certain expenses that enhance a disabled person's quality of life—from residential treatment programs to movie tickets or haircuts—without cutting off access to government benefits, such as Medicaid or Supplemental Security Income (SSI), the latter administered by the Social Security Administration.

Government payments can cover much of a disabled person's expenses. But in order to qualify for them, individuals cannot have assets in their own names that exceed $2,000 (not including a home, a vehicle and basic personal items). In 1993, Congress permitted special-needs individuals under age 65 to have trusts funded with their own money—such as assets from a legal settlement or an inheritance—and still have access to government benefits. More common, however, are so-called third-party trusts, in which parents fund trusts for their children.

Funds transferred to a trust are not considered to be assets of the special-needs individual, as long as there's an independent trustee who controls distributions of the money and the disabled person can't just grab cash from the trust at will. A trust also ensures that a qualified individual will be watching over the money, a particular concern for families since many disabled individuals cannot manage money on their own.

Barry Nelson, a Miami lawyer, set up a special-needs trust for his autistic son, Jesse, now a teenager. The trust will be funded by life insurance when Nelson dies, and can be used to pay for expenses beyond what Medicaid or SSI would pay for, including "travel, companionship and cultural experiences" and "purchase of small visual and/or audio equipment for entertainment purposes," such as iPods or DVD players, according to the trust document. A special-needs trust "gives me—and it gives every parent—peace of mind," said Nelson, who said medical and educational expenses for his son run between $50,000 and $100,000 a year.

Rules governing special-needs trusts are complicated and vary by state and by the source of the funds. Relatives or parents themselves can be the trustees of the funds, although some experts recommend naming a financial services company or a trusted adviser, such as a lawyer or accountant, to help manage the money and make distributions.

Ideally, the trustee should communicate regularly with the disabled person and be able to work closely with doctors, therapists and a slew of government agencies. Trustees also need to be very careful when making distributions. For instance, they should avoid paying money directly to the person with special needs, since that may disqualify him or her for government benefits.

It's also crucial for grandparents and other relatives to retool their own estate plans to leave gifts or inheritances to the special-needs trust, rather than directly to the person with disabilities, in order to preserve eligibility for government programs. Beneficiary designations on retirement accounts and life insurance policies should also go to the trust.

"You've got to make sure that the relatives' estate plans are coordinated," said Sebastian V. Grassi Jr., a Troy, Michigan, estate-planning lawyer. He created a special-needs trust for his daughter, who has cerebral palsy.

Another option are "pooled" trusts, in which funds from many special-needs families are bundled together and managed by non-profit groups that focus on disability issues. Families typically use pooled trusts if they can't find appropriate individual or bank trustees, or if they have a small trust account that would benefit from being bunched with those of other families.

## WHERE TO GO FOR HELP

A growing number of financial-services companies, lawyers and financial planners are offering services for families with disabilities. Here are some resources:

- **MetLife Center for Special Needs Planning** (www.metlife.com/specialneeds). MetLife offers insurance products, financial advice and resources for families with disabilities. The website also features a cost-of-care calculator.

- **MassMutual Financial Group's SpecialCare Unit** (www.massmutual.com/specialcare). This program provides financial products and advice for special-needs families. Agents get special training in disability planning.

- **Academy of Special Needs Planners** (www.specialneedsanswers.com). A professional group of lawyers knowledgeable about estate planning, government benefits and other disability-related concerns.

- **Special Needs Alliance** (www.specialneedsalliance.org). This nonprofit group provides referrals to experienced special-needs lawyers and other disability resources.

There are some other key steps families with special needs should take. Parents should create power-of-attorney or guardianship documents for finances and health care, naming themselves as their child's agent or guardian when their child turns 18. Without this formality, parents of kids over 18 may not be able to have access to their child's medical records or make health care or financial decisions.

It's also smart to create a "letter of guidance," a document spelling out everything another caregiver should know about their child's special needs, including medical diagnosis, treatment and medications, as well as specific likes or dislikes and food preferences or aversions. "You know things about your children that no one else on this earth knows," said Michael Gilfix, a Palo Alto, California, lawyer who does a lot of special-needs planning. "This includes little things, like what breakfast food makes them happy or what breakfast food makes them really angry."

Valentine, a client of Gilfix, wrote a letter of guidance for her son, Gabe. The document describes how Gabe is a huge San Francisco Giants fan, so any caregiver should make sure he gets tickets to home games. He doesn't like ice cream or cake but does like pizza. This may seem trivial, but to children whose condition makes it difficult for them to express themselves, these kinds of details can have a huge impact on quality of life. Gabe's epilepsy medication affects his teeth, so his mother's letter recommends that he get his teeth cleaned regularly. "He actually loves the dentist," she said.

## ADVANCE MEDICAL DIRECTIVES AND "LIVING WILLS"

Advance medical directives detail the kind of medical care that you would want in case you are incapacitated and can't voice your own wishes. Of course, medical directives can't cover all of the potential what-ifs and medical gray areas that can arise. But they're a good start.

An "advance medical directive" typically has two parts: a health care proxy and a living will. The "health care proxy," or durable power of attorney for health care, designates a person, such as a spouse or trusted friend, who can legally act as your agent, making medical decisions for you if you are incapacitated. (You can also name a team of people, such as your siblings, to serve as your health care proxies, but beware that they may disagree, causing family discord.)

Meanwhile, the "living will" portion describes the type of care you would want if you become critically ill and spells out what you want or don't want in terms of end-of-life care.

End-of-life guidelines are as much for the living as for the dying. Without specific instructions, family members may have to decide whether you would want to be kept alive artificially, what level of disability you'd be willing to live with and how to let you die if you had no hope of recovery. (My family had to deal with these tough decisions when my great-aunt was terminally ill and left no end-of-life instructions; I can tell you that deciding what to do is incredibly challenging.)

Still, less than a third of Americans adults, and less than half of nursing home patients, have created these documents, according to studies.

Living wills are important to communicate to your loved ones your feelings about what kind of life is worth living. They can be critical if family members don't agree on your treatment. That's what happened in the high-profile case of Terri Schiavo; in a protracted legal battle, her husband requested to have her feeding tube removed, while her parents sought to keep her alive. The feeding tube was ultimately removed in 2005. Had she clearly spelled out her own wishes in an advance directive, the heated family battle might have been avoided.

The laws governing these documents vary by state, including rules about who can and cannot be a witness when the documents are signed, so make sure you get state-specific forms. For instance, New York requires two witnesses for health care proxy documents—but the person you have named as your health care agent or backup agent can't be one of them. Such documents are widely available online or through hospitals or state medical or bar associations. If you have homes in multiple states, check with your lawyer to make sure your medical directives comply with laws in all those states.

The National Hospice and Palliative Care Organization's Caring Connections website has all fifty state forms available for free at www.caringinfo.org/stateaddownload. Five Wishes is a simpler version that meets the legal requirements in some forty states; it's available from www.agingwithdignity.org for a small fee.

Some forms simply ask if a person does or doesn't want life-prolonging treatment if he or she is considered terminal or unlikely to regain consciousness. Some ask whether a person would want specific life-prolonging treatments, including ventilators, artificial nutrition, kidney dialysis and artificial resuscitation. Sometimes the directives can contain non-medical instructions. One lawyer said his clients had specific instructions regarding grooming or certain music and fresh flowers in their rooms in the event of hospitalization. You can also specify whether you'd want to take part in experimental procedures.

Before signing the documents, it's wise to check with a lawyer to make sure you know the proper witnessing requirements and that the document clearly expresses your wishes. Many people have religious considerations about end-of-life decisions or organ donations, for instance, that might not be reflected in a generic state form.

Also be sure your agent has authorization to access medical records under the Health Insurance Portability and Accountability Act (HIPAA). This 1996 law, designed to protect patient privacy, requires that health care providers limit the release of your medical information, so you need to expressly authorize your agent to view your medical history.

Advance directives do not need to be filed officially. They go into effect automatically as soon as they are signed and witnessed; some states also require notarization. Once the documents are signed, give copies to your doctors, your hospital, your agent (and backup agent) and other family members or close confidantes, or at least give instructions on how to find them. One study found that in 50% of cases, the forms were tucked in the patient's safe-deposit box and inaccessible when they were needed.

Some states have electronic registries that store advance directives online and make them accessible to health care providers via a password and give patients wallet cards. Google Health has started a similar online service at www.google.com/intl/en/health/advance-directive.html.

Make sure to sit down and talk about your wishes with the person you have named as your agent, lawyers say. These talks are anything but easy, which is why so many of us procrastinate. In doing so, you need to address such questions as "Would you want to live in a persistent vegetative state with a feeding tube, despite the long-term costs?" or "Would you rather that the tube be withdrawn, in which case you'll die of starvation?" The best time to begin is when you are in good health, when the discussion can be hypothetical. Aging with Dignity's Next Steps booklet (www.agingwithdignity.org) offers advice on how to begin the conversation with loved ones, such as mentioning your own end-of-life preferences or discussing the forms at a group family meeting.

Estate planners and doctors encourage people to periodically refresh their health care directives. If your health care proxy agent dies, gets sick or moves away, you will need to designate someone else. Living wills also need to take into account medical advances that can turn what once was a terminal or irreversible condition into something treatable.

## ORGAN DONATIONS

If you are interested in being an organ donor, you should make sure to carry a card that designates you as such in your wallet at all times. Driver's licenses typically include information about your wishes for organ donations.

You can find forms expressing your donation intentions at www.donatelife.net. You or your lawyer can also prepare a form as part of your advance medical directives that lists the organs you would like donated; check with legal authorities in your state about witnessing requirements and notarizations, since rules vary.

It's also key to tell loved ones about your intentions regarding organ donations. If an organ isn't preserved shortly after death, your wishes may not be able to be fulfilled.

And if you feel strongly against organ donations, make sure to make those views known, too, either in your health care directives or in an accompanying letter in your estate plan.

# FUNERAL ARRANGEMENTS AND DISPOSITION OF REMAINS

Almost everyone, at some point, has imagined their own funeral. Will there be throngs of people singing your praises? Will exes show up, uncontrollably weeping? When you're creating your estate plan, it's also time to think seriously about these final arrangements.

It's smart to provide as much guidance as you can about your funeral arrangements, to prevent disputes down the road. Some families disagree bitterly about cremation, autopsies, burials and organ donations, because of deeply held religious or cultural beliefs. Should you be buried in your family's plot or your spouse's? Open or closed casket? What sort of clergy should preside over the funeral, if you have a diverse religious background? Should you donate your body to science?

If you have strong feelings, it's best to make them known ahead of time in a letter to your survivors or to your agent, in case you become incapacitated. The more decisions you can make about your final arrangements ahead of time, the easier it is for your grieving survivors. Talk to your lawyer and your local funeral home about how best to specify arrangements ahead of time.

In many states, you can also designate an "agent for body disposition," which is different from conferring a health care power of attorney. This agent specifies what should be done with your remains. Typically, that role goes to your next of kin, but if you would rather someone else handle the job, be sure to name such an agent.

Some people also prepay funeral arrangements, so the burden isn't left to their survivors—but beware of high-pressure sales tactics, lost contracts and inflexible arrangements if you later move. (The costs of your funeral are also deductible from your gross estate for tax purposes.)

Federal regulations require funeral homes to provide written price lists, so you can compare costs. The Federal Trade Commission has a consumer planning guide for funerals on its website; go to www.ftc.gov and type "funerals" in the search box. Another helpful resource is the Funeral Consumers Alliance (www.funerals.org), which can help you determine funeral procedures and regulations where you live. The AARP also has useful information on planning your funeral on its website, www.aarp.org.

### A DEEPER LOOK
## ESTATE PLANNING FOR PET OWNERS

Irene Wright set up a detailed trust to care for her loved ones when she becomes unable to care for them. However, her estate plan isn't for her children, it's for her two papillon dogs and her seven cats.

"I just wanted to make sure that they would be cared for and they wouldn't be orphans," said Wright, a retired accountant. Her plan includes a panel of family members and friends who have legal oversight over the animals' care, and a dedicated caretaker who will handle the day-to-day care.

A growing number of states and jurisdictions are recognizing the importance of pet estate planning by passing legislation allowing for trusts that directly benefit a pet, rather than a human. State statutes vary, and some have set term limits for trusts, which may not work if you have a pet, such as a parrot, that typically has a long life span. Even if your state doesn't have a pet trust statute, you can always leave money in trust for a person, with detailed provisions that he or she use the money to care for the pet.

How much to leave for your pet depends on the type, age, health and lifestyle of the animal. Lawyers recommend calculating how much you typically spend on your pet per year and multiplying that by the estimated life expectancy of the animal. Courts may be able to reduce the amount you leave for your pet in trust if a judge deems it excessive.

Instead of a trust, some owners put a provision in their wills that leaves the pet—and typically some money to care for the pet—to a relative or friend. The problem, lawyers say, is that such arrangements may not be enforceable. Heirs may decide they don't want to take responsibility for the pet, or become unable to care for it. Once the animal is given to the caregiver under the will, there's no further supervision.

A pet trust has more teeth than simply providing for a pet in your will. That's because it allows you to set out specific funds for your pet's well-being and name both a caregiver who will handle the pet's care and a trustee who will manage the funds and make sure the pet is taken care of. (Naming different people as caregiver and trustee allows for checks and balances.) Provisions in a trust are generally enforceable by a court. Make sure to name alternative caregivers and trustees in case your first choices can't, or won't, serve in the role. When the pet dies, the money in the trust goes to remainder beneficiaries, typically a family member, friend or charity.

If there are no individuals to whom you would entrust your pet, you can leave the animal in the care of a pet sanctuary or retirement home, which will watch over it until it dies, usually in exchange for a sizable donation. These kinds of arrangements are typically sponsored by university veterinary schools or non-profit animal welfare groups. Check with your local humane society or vet schools in your area to see if they offer such programs, and be sure to make arrangements with the program before putting it in your estate plan.

Leaving a pet to a university veterinary school pet care program can get very pricey. Some programs suggest minimum contributions of $10,000 or $25,000 per pet, with even heftier costs for larger animals, such as horses, or pets with

## PLANNING FOR FIDO'S CARE

The following websites provide more details on how you can create an estate plan for your pets.

- www.professorbeyer.com/Articles/Animals.htm, the website of a law school professor who has written extensively about pet trusts

- www.2ndchance4pets.org, a non-profit that helps make sure your pets are taken care of when you can't

- www.aspca.org, provides information on pet trusts (search for "pet trust" on the site)

- www.humanesociety.org, the website of the Humane Society of the United States, with information on planning for your pet's future without you

special needs. Upon the animal's death, the contribution becomes property of the school.

Anne-Marie Schiro created a trust for the care of her four cats because she was concerned that they would outlive her. The trust outlines that the North Shore Animal League, an animal sanctuary in Port Washington, New York, care for the pets. Schiro met with the animal sanctuary before drafting the trust, and in exchange for a $12,500 contribution, they agreed to care for the cats after her death or incapacity.

Advisers suggest leaving instructions in your estate plan that are as detailed as possible, including your pet's likes, dislikes and idiosyncrasies, to help ensure that your pet will be cared for as you wish. Also, don't forget to leave instructions for the pet's burial or cremation.

Lawyers also recommend setting up power-of-attorney documents that specifically allow your appointed agent to make financial decisions regarding your pet if you become incapacitated. Many animal welfare groups also provide wallet cards or stickers letting others know, in the case of an emergency, that you have a pet that needs care.

## CHAPTER 9

# PRESERVING FAMILY HARMONY

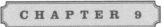

We've all heard about estate plans that have gone awry. The news regularly features stories of heirs to large fortunes battling over the estates of a wealthy family member, and many great novels, such as Charles Dickens' *Bleak House,* are based on such tales.

But many of these fractious family dramas can be prevented. In this chapter, I'll go over some ways to bulletproof your documents to help prevent family feuds and legal challenges when you're no longer around to voice your wishes. I'll discuss tactics for divvying up your tangible personal possessions fairly, an issue that's often the root of major family disputes. I'll talk about planning for "blended families"—in other words, how to divide your assets if you are in a re-marriage. (I covered other strategies to help maintain family harmony—including how to balance out gifts and bequests to heirs who may have very different economic circumstances—and how to disinherit someone, in Chapter Three.) And because the time-consuming task of caring for an incapacitated family member can lead to family friction, in "A Deeper Look," I'll discuss "caregiving contracts," in which you pay children for their caregiving duties.

Most estate challenges arise when an estate plan isn't

communicated properly or when an estate is divvied up unequally among heirs. Challenges usually take the following
tacks: someone may argue that you were unduly influenced
by a third party (typically the favored heir), that you weren't
of sound mind when you drafted your plans or that mistakes
were made when the will was drafted.

A contested will or estate feud can place your assets in legal limbo and leech money in legal fees from your rightful
beneficiaries. (Read *Bleak House* for a heartbreaking example.) So it's smart to take preventative measures to help avoid
such situations.

## EXPRESS YOUR WISHES— AND PROVE YOUR CAPACITY

First and foremost, whenever possible, you should be open
about your inheritance plan while you are still alive, so every
family member truly understands it, minimizing the chances
for suspicions to arise later.

It's also wise to elaborate the reasons behind your estate
plan, especially if you are making uneven distributions to your
heirs. That can help ensure there isn't a chance of misinter-
preting your estate-planning documents. If you can explain
exactly why one child is getting the house and another the
family silver, for example, the children are less likely to challenge the decision later.

If you don't want to have this admittedly difficult conversation while you're alive, you can write a letter or make a video
elaborating the reasons and thought process behind your
plan and making it clear that these decisions are yours alone.
You can clarify certain estate-planning decisions, such as giving your heirs unequal inheritances or even disinheriting
someone. You can also express your values or your hopes and
dreams for heirs, in what are often termed "ethical wills." (I
touched on ethical wills in Chapter Three.) These documents

can accompany your will as attached memoranda, to be read or viewed upon your death.

These measures are also important in preventing charges of "undue influence." That's when an elderly or incapacitated person is coerced by a not-so-well-meaning friend or relative, sometimes criminally, to create an estate plan benefitting the unscrupulous individual.

It's generally not smart, however, to videotape the actual will or trust signing in order to prove you're of sound mind. A litigating heir could hire a forensic psychologist who may interpret a quiver or an absentminded remark as a sign of incapacity.

It's interesting that the legal standard for the mental capacity required to create a will, or what estate planners call "testamentary capacity," isn't that high. Although each state has different standards for testamentary capacity, you generally need to know what your property is, how you want to distribute it and who your relatives are.

If there's any question about your capacity at the time you make or update your estate plans, take steps to prove it. Some lawyers will test you themselves for capacity, using simple, standard tests, such as the Mini-Mental State Examination, or will have you see a doctor to assess your mental state.

Another tactic to prove capacity is to draft a series of new estate-planning documents every few months. Each document should be slightly different from the previous one (such as giving a small amount of money to a new charity) but should have roughly the same intent in terms of how major property is distributed. Serial wills can demonstrate that you reviewed the will each time but chose not to change the primary distribution of property on a whim. If the estate plan is contested, challengers would essentially have to find each of the serial documents invalid, which could be a lengthy and expensive process.

As I addressed in the previous chapter, a loved one or an heir has some recourse if you suspect that an estate plan has been subject to undue influence. If you sense wrongdoing, contact your local district attorney's office, many of which have elder-abuse units, and let them investigate. You can also petition a court to name a protective guardian or conservator for a family member. Typically, court-appointed guardians can be another relative or a third party, such as a lawyer, a bank, a social worker or a specially trained professional guardian.

## SAFEGUARDS TO PREVENT CONFLICT

There are also a number of safeguards that you can include in your estate plan to help minimize conflict. For instance, some people include clauses in their wills and/or trusts stipulating that any future disputes be settled through mediation or arbitration, rather than costly litigation.

"Mediation" is when disputing parties hire a middleman to help them negotiate a settlement. Mediators don't make decisions; they simply help families reach an agreement. Mediation is typically less contentious, more private and less expensive than court proceedings. Caveats: mediators' qualifications vary widely, and the technique can be less effective if one party is richer or more powerful than another.

"Arbitration," meanwhile, is when families choose a third party who makes decisions about contested issues. The process is still generally faster, less costly and more private than court proceedings. The downside is that decisions are generally binding and hard to appeal.

Some wills and trusts even include "no-contest" clauses (*in terrorem* clauses in legalese), which actually disinherit heirs who attempt to challenge the documents. Michael Jackson's estate, for instance, included such a clause. No-contest clauses can be a good idea if you plan to give to your heirs unequally, because heirs who feel shortchanged might hesitate to dispute if it could mean losing everything. However, such clauses may not be upheld in court in a number of states, such as Florida, so check with a lawyer where you live.

If using a no-contest clause, it's smart not to disinherit heirs completely. That's because if heirs are left nothing, there's no downside to challenging the estate plan. But when heirs receive some inheritance, they have more at risk if they contest the plans.

If you do anticipate that some heirs will feel slighted by your estate plan, you may also want to consider naming an adviser or bank as your estate executor or trustee, to avoid placing family members in the awkward position of having to make disbursements to other relatives.

### A DEEPER LOOK
## PLANNING FOR BLENDED FAMILIES

One of the thorniest estate-planning situations is how to split up assets—and keep the peace—when you're in a new marriage and have children from a previous relationship. More than half of U.S. families are remarried or blended, according to Census data, and some 1,300 new stepfamilies are formed daily.

Decisions may be complicated by the emotional tensions among parents, stepparents, stepsiblings, half siblings and the like. You want to make sure that you provide properly for a new spouse or child and that the plan doesn't cause division or litigation. The last thing you want is your kids from a previous marriage suing your new spouse for a piece of the wealth.

So what steps can you take to help maintain harmony? Of course, as I keep on stressing, the most important thing is clear communication with family members. Be open—with your financial advisers and, if possible, with your family—about the reasoning behind your decisions. If relations with certain family members or exes are too strained to have such discussions, make sure the rationale behind your decisions is clear in the estate-planning documents and with your estate advisers.

There are also some specific structures you can set up to help keep the peace. Here are some tips.

## Pre- and Postnuptial Agreements

While prenups and postnups may not exactly be the most romantic topics to bring up, they are really valuable when you want to ensure that your kids from a previous marriage will be protected. (Prenuptial agreements are set up before marriage; couples who have already tied the knot should consider setting up a postnuptial agreement.)

These agreements can be used for estate planning by designating whether assets are considered marital or separate property. For instance, one partner can waive rights to property, such as a vacation home, that the other partner would like to have go to his or her children. Or a couple could spell out whether certain savings should go to their separate children, while also setting aside a separate pot of money for the kids they plan to have together. Some retirement plans may require a spouse's consent to give the plan's assets to anyone but the spouse, such as children from a previous marriage; a prenup or postnup may be used to provide such consent.

Make sure each spouse hires a lawyer individually who is familiar with the laws where you live, since rules vary by state.

## QTIPs

A qualified terminable interest property trust, otherwise known as a QTIP, is a kind of trust often used by blended families to provide regular income for a spouse while preserving assets for the children of a prior marriage. (I introduced QTIPs previously in Chapter Five.)

Traditionally, in a QTIP, the investment income from the trust was distributed at least annually to the surviving spouse, while the principal in the trust went to the kids from a first marriage, usually upon the surviving spouse's death.

That arrangement sometimes led to fights between children and the surviving stepparent over how trust assets were invested. The stepparent often wanted the trust to generate more income, while the children wanted the trust to accrue more principal appreciation.

Now, though, there are steps you can take to prevent such disputes. You can give an independent trustee the authority to adjust between principal and income, depending on the investment climate and family circumstances, in order to treat beneficiaries fairly. Also, you can use what's called a unitrust, which gives your surviving spouse a set percentage of the trust's assets, rather than simply the investment income.

## Life Estates

A "life estate" is very useful tool for ensuring that loved ones don't fight over who gets to live in your home after you die. Let's say you're married to your second wife but have kids from your previous marriage. Upon your death, you can give your second wife a life estate, or the right to live in and enjoy your home, but only for the remainder of her lifetime.

Upon her death, the property passes to the beneficiaries (typically your kids from your first marriage) whom you set out in your will, trust or prenuptial or postnuptial agreements. In some cases, the property is transferred not at death but earlier, if your surviving spouse, say, must enter an assisted-living facility. Rules concerning the taxation of life estates can vary by state.

## Life Insurance

Insurance policies can be a great tool for blended families. Life insurance can be used, for instance, as a way to equalize assets. You can name your kids from a prior marriage to be the beneficiaries of the life insurance policy, while leaving your home and other assets to your current spouse and any children you have together.

## Beneficiary Designations

If you divorce, it's crucial that your beneficiary designations on your retirement plans, life insurance and bank and investment accounts are up to date. If you don't change your beneficiary designation to reflect your divorce or your new marriage, your ex-spouse could very well receive your retirement plan assets.

In fact, the U.S. Supreme Court, in a 2008 ruling, *Kennedy v. Plan Administrator*, unanimously ruled that the plan administrator must follow the directions in its own plan documents, which includes beneficiary forms.

So make sure to remove ex-spouses as beneficiaries on retirement accounts, life insurance policies, and ownership documents of bank accounts, real estate and vehicles, if that's your wish. Also make sure to update your will to reflect a divorce or remarriage.

## Tangible Personal Property

Family heirlooms, such as antiques, jewelry or photos, especially those that have been in the family for a long time, can be one of the most contested facets of an estate plan, as I discussed earlier. But feelings can be especially raw if such objects end up outside of the family—say, with a second spouse. Some lawyers suggest giving away family heirlooms during your lifetime, so you can supervise who gets what and why—and to help prevent a free-for-all over such objects later on.

### A DEEPER LOOK
## DEALING WITH PERSONAL PROPERTY

The process of distributing a family's tangible belongings— often mundane knickknacks with far more sentimental value than monetary worth—has ignited many a family feud.

Divorce and second marriages can add to the tension, as children and stepfamilies vie for valued objects.

Estate lawyer Steven Oshins once administered a $2 million estate in which a widower and his stepson had a big fight over a piece of property. No, it wasn't the house or the stock portfolio. It was a toaster oven. He estimated the heirs ran up some $3,000 in legal fees fighting over that appliance. "The value of the asset isn't the issue," he said. "It's making sure the other person doesn't get it."

Poor advance planning can increase the likelihood of friction. In many wills, parents simply leave their possessions to their children without specifying who gets what. Also, people often make informal, oral promises to heirs over the years. This is asking for trouble.

Roswell, Georgia, estate lawyer John Scroggin said one of his clients told her son that he would receive the family's grandfather clock. But she also promised the same clock to her daughter. After the mother died, the son started carting the clock out of the house. When the daughter saw this, the two siblings ended up in a fistfight, breaking the clock in the process. Now, several years later, the siblings still don't speak, and no one got the clock.

Moreover, if there are no specific instructions as to who gets what, greedy heirs or their spouses may filch objects before the estate is fully accounted for and other heirs have a chance to check out the items. "I've gotten to the point that we will go in when someone dies and get the locks changed almost immediately," Scroggin said.

But there are a number of creative strategies, including "family auctions" and a "round-robin" selection strategy, to divide tangible property without splitting families apart.

As a first step, estate planners recommend that families get together while everyone is still in good health to talk about who wants what. If more than one heir wants the same thing, the parents can have the ultimate say. This also gives parents a chance to explain the history of family heirlooms so the stories behind the objects aren't lost.

"The ideal is having the conversation in advance, asking kids what they want and why, and finding out what is meaningful," said Marlene Stum, professor of family social science at the University of Minnesota, who has conducted research on property distribution. As I mentioned in Chapter One, the university has created a program called Who Gets Grandma's Yellow Pie Plate? which includes a detailed workbook, video and website, http://yellowpieplate.umn.edu, with pointers to help families discuss property distribution. For instance, some families take into account a child's caregiving contributions, economic status or family situation when determining how to divvy up property.

It's smart to formalize the decisions either in a will or as a separate personal property list that's referenced in the will. In this list, called a "personal property memorandum," you can even spell out whether you want a certain asset sold, having your heirs split the windfall. Make sure to update these as circumstances change. (Requirements for personal property lists vary by state, so check with a lawyer where you live.) Some families also draw up side letters or videos that further explain their intentions.

Some nice benefits of personal property memorandums are that they are typically more informal and private than your will. So you might be able to change who gets your photo collection without going through the formal process of updating a will, or sometimes without the public scrutiny of a probated document. However, in some states, personal property memorandums simply serve as guidance for executors and aren't necessarily binding instructions.

With parents living longer, many want to start unloading their stuff while they are still alive. But make sure that the giver's intentions are clear and consistent with other estate-planning documents, so other heirs don't doubt the transaction later on. Also beware that such transfers while living may be considered taxable gifts. (On a related note, if you do want to give away property while still alive, you should try to actually physically transfer your property to your heirs, rather than keep it in your house; otherwise it may still be considered part of your estate upon your death.)

Some families turn to a round-robin strategy, said Paramus, New Jersey, lawyer Martin Shenkman. Heirs draw straws and whoever wins gets first choice of items they would like to have, often in a particular room. On each round, a different heir gets to choose first. Some families decide to appraise the items beforehand so that each family member is aware of the value of the assets they choose.

Another tactic is for either the parent or the children to label objects in order to designate who gets what. But beware that labels can fall off or can be moved by unscrupulous heirs.

Lawyer Olivia Birnbaum said her grandmother invited her five children home to tag what they wanted. (Each child got a different color tag, and spouses and children stayed home.) "If they wanted to fight over a vase, that was the time," said Birnbaum. Using the tags as a guide, her grandmother then made a list of how the objects were to be divided. "Everyone still speaks to each other," added Birnbaum.

Another option is to hold a private "family auction." Some families hold silent auctions, in which family members submit bids on assets they want but don't see what other heirs bid. The highest bid price is then deducted from the bidder's inheritance. Estate planners say that auctions are generally highly effective as long as everyone agrees to the rules beforehand.

David Altshuler's family decided to try an auction. After his physician father died a few years ago in Denver, his mother requested that he and his two siblings divide most of their father's stuff. The siblings spent a weekend in Denver picking out objects they wanted. Most items weren't contested. But there were thirty-seven pieces, such as their father's silver-striped wedding tie and a 1971 white Buick Riviera, that more than one sibling desired.

Altshuler's solution was to hold a "sentimental auction," so called because many of the pieces auctioned had little

## DISTRIBUTING PERSONAL OBJECTS

- **Gather family members to talk about who wants what** while everyone is still in good health. If more than one heir wants the same thing, the parents can have the ultimate say.

- **The University of Minnesota** has created a detailed workbook, video and website (www.yellowpieplate.umn.edu) with pointers to help families hold these discussions.

- **Fair doesn't always mean equal.** Some families take into account caregiving contributions, economic status or family situations when determining how to distribute property. What's fair may not result in an equal split.

- **Formalize property distribution decisions** either in a will or as a separate personal property list that's referenced in the will. Some families also draw up side letters or videos that further explain their intentions.

- **Some families choose to tag objects** with labels in order to designate who gets what.

- **Other families hold "sentimental auctions"** in which family members bid on objects using virtual points rather than real money.

- **Another alternative is a round-robin process** in which family members take turns picking out items they would like to have.

economic worth but were rich in sentimental value. Instead of using cash, each heir received ten thousand "virtual points" to spend. "If we had brought cash into it, it would not have felt as fair," Altshuler said.

Armed with a digital camera and PowerPoint, the siblings created a digital catalog of the disputed items. Several weeks later, the siblings, who all lived in different states, logged onto their computers. Using WebEx, an online communication tool used by companies to hold virtual meetings, the siblings bid with their points for the items. The whole auction took about two hours.

In order to minimize any problems, the siblings set some rules. For instance, only the three siblings could bid, but their bids could be on behalf of their spouses and children. Some issues were still unresolved: there was one item—their dad's army shirt—that both Altshuler and his brother were willing to bid their entire point cache for. They ended up removing it from the auction and placing it in the hands of the executor. (They have considered rotating possession of it every few years in a "joint custody" arrangement.)

Altshuler successfully bid for his father's wedding tie, using 7,600 of his 10,000 points, while his brother got the Buick.

"Dealing with an estate is an emotional minefield," said Altshuler. "This kind of process can make a real contribution to family happiness," he said.

## A DEEPER LOOK
## CAREGIVING CONTRACTS TO EQUALIZE ESTATES

Trish Richert signed a binding employment contract. In exchange for taking care of an elderly woman—arranging and taking her to doctors' appointments, doing her bills, keeping her house tidy—Richert received a modest stipend that covered travel expenses and other costs.

Richert's employer: her mother. The two entered into a so-called caregiver contract—a formal agreement, set up by a lawyer—in which Richert received a small payment for the long hours she spent caring for her mom.

A growing number of families are setting up caregiver contracts, in which adult children or other relatives are hired, for modest salaries, to take care of elderly or disabled family members. These arrangements, which are also called personal-service or personal-care agreements, can minimize battles between siblings and other family members. For many other families, the contracts simply help reward the significant amounts of time, effort and money that family members often spend watching over and taking care of an elderly relative.

Advisers and family members say the deals are smart because a formal arrangement, done ahead of time, can minimize feuds among siblings and other relatives. Oftentimes, one child serves as a primary caregiver and a parent may reward him or her by making informal gifts or by doling out a bigger piece of the estate in the will. Unfortunately, those arrangements can lead to family fights or will contests.

A formal caregiver contract, drafted ahead of time, makes the arrangement "more ironclad," said New York elder law attorney Bernard Krooks. "You have a written document showing this is what Mom wants you to do and what Mom wants to do for you. It helps avoid family squabbles." But lawyers say it's important to discuss the contract with other siblings or relatives so they are aware of the arrangement ahead of time; that can help minimize family tensions later.

Caregiver contracts can also help reduce the size of a parent's estate and thereby improve his or her chances of becoming eligible for long-term-care coverage under Medicaid. Legislation passed several years ago made it tougher to qualify for Medicaid long-term-care coverage by making outright gifts to family members. These measures were taken to prevent seniors who have the means to pay for their own care from obtaining Medicaid, which is intended for poor patients. Lawyers say that if set up properly, caregiver contracts shouldn't be considered gifts to children because the patient is receiving a real service in return.

Still, there's a lot of stigma to overcome when recommending the idea to families, lawyers say. The main reason: people are still uncomfortable with the idea of paying their kids. So while caregiver contracts can be a smart move, they aren't right for every family, especially those who find paying their kids too awkward.

Indeed, when Richert first heard about the contracts from her mother's lawyer, A. Frank Johns, "it felt funny," she said. "It's hard to put a dollar figure when you are doing something for your mom."

Terry Huffines set up a caregiver contract with her elderly aunt, to help avoid any estate problems down the road with her aunt's fifteen additional nieces and nephews. The agreement, set up by Johns, her lawyer, outlined the services Huffines would provide for her aunt, including driving her to the doctor and the grocery store and doing other household chores.

In order for a caregiver contract to be legally respected— and to pass muster with Medicaid authorities—it has to follow certain formalities. For one, you can't pay the caregiver an inflated rate in order to shift lots of money out of your estate. Instead, you should specify what duties the caregiver is expected to perform and then contact local home care agencies or geriatric care managers to establish the market value of those services in your area. Such duties can vary from preparing meals to bathing and dressing, housecleaning, chauffeuring, arranging doctor's appointments and friends' visits and overseeing medications.

The cost of care varies widely, depending on location and the services being performed, and can range from about $15 an hour to more than $100 an hour. Some families choose to pay a discounted rate to family caregivers, which is also acceptable, lawyers say. It's also much better to set up the caregiver contract when the incapacitated adult is of sound mind, as the arrangements can become far more complicated if a person with power of attorney signs the contract.

The contract should also specify whether the payment will be done in one up-front lump sum based on the senior's life expectancy—a technique often used for Medicaid planning— or in regular weekly or monthly payments.

There are also tax consequences to consider. The compensation is considered ordinary income, so the caregiver has to pay income taxes on the payment. Also, depending on how the contract is structured, Social Security and other payroll taxes may have to be withheld.

It's wise to check whether there are other sources of funding you can use to pay family members. Some long-term-care insurance policies, such as those that pay lump sum indemnity benefits, may be used to pay family members who provide care. If you already have a policy or are considering one, see if the coverage will allow you to pay family members for their caregiving services.

In addition, some state or federal government programs provide funding to compensate family members in what is known as "consumer-directed care." For instance, a growing number of states have a Cash & Counseling program for Medicaid enrollees that allows participants to pay family members for their services. Contact your local agency on aging or department of social services for more information on government funding.

## TAKING CARE

These websites offer information on caregiving contracts or related issues:

- National Academy of Elder Law Attorneys (www.naela.com)

- American Bar Association Commission on Law and Aging (www.abanet.org/aging)

- National Family Caregivers Association (www.thefamilycaregiver.org)

- Family Caregiver Alliance (www.caregiver.org)

- National Alliance for Caregiving (www.caregiving.org)

## DEFUSING FAMILY FEUDS

There are many steps a family can take to reduce the likelihood of a fight over money. Some tips:

- Be open about an inheritance plan so every family member truly understands it, minimizing the chances that suspicions will arise.

- Try to ensure a plan won't be misinterpreted. After discussing your intentions, create a video or write a letter explaining the reasoning behind your decisions.

- Be careful about videotaping actual will or trust signings. Sometimes a quiver or a dropped name could be interpreted as a sign of incapacity.

- Build safeguards into your estate plan to help minimize conflict, such as a clause recommending mediation, rather than litigation, to resolve disputes, or a no-contest clause to disinherit heirs who challenge provisions. (Laws vary by state, so ask your lawyer what options are available for your situation.)

- Consider naming an adviser or bank as estate executor or trustee, to avoid placing family members in the awkward position of disbursing money to other relatives.

- Set up a round-robin process to divide property. Have children take turns picking out items they would like to have. On each round, a different child goes first. Those who take items of less worth may get compensated with cash.

- When two family members want the same asset, hold a silent auction. Family members bid on assets they want, and the highest bid price is deducted from the bidder's inheritance.

- Consider a caregiver contract, in which you reimburse family members for their time-intensive caregiving duties.

## CHAPTER 10

# MAINTAINING
# YOUR PLAN

OK, now you have an estate plan. You've carefully pre-pared your will. You've divvied up your personal prop-erty. You've created a trust to benefit your spouse and your children. You've written up advance medical directives and power-of-attorney documents for health care and finances. You've designated a guardian for your kids. In short, you're all set. Right?

Well, not exactly. That's because an estate plan, like life itself, is fluid. It needs to change as your circumstances change—as you get married or divorced, have children or grandchildren, move to a different state or grow closer or farther apart from relatives and friends, and as loved ones become ill or pass away. What's more, your wealth waxes and wanes, you buy and sell property and make large gifts to char-ity, and through it all, tax and estate-planning laws are con-stantly in flux (as the ever-changing laws in recent years have demonstrated).

As these events happen, your estate plan must be updated to reflect current circumstances. It's also crucial, as we talk about below, to store your estate plan carefully and let loved ones know how to access it when the time comes. In this con-cluding chapter, I'll go over the "care and feeding" of your estate plan—how to store it and when to update it.

Of course, certain vehicles, such as many trusts or completed charitable gifts, are irrevocable, which means they can't be taken back. But as long as you are of sound capacity, you can adjust many other things, such as your will, guardianship designations for your kids, revocable living trusts, health care directives and power-of-attorney documents.

As you update your estate plan, it's key to communicate any major changes to your loved ones, to prevent any unwelcome surprises and to help deter the family fights that can erupt when people are unprepared to deal with estate plans. As I've stressed throughout the book, open communication about your estate plans is the best way to ensure family harmony during *and* after your lifetime.

## STORING YOUR ESTATE PLAN

You've gone through all the hard work of creating a detailed estate plan. But all this effort is pretty much useless if no one can find it when the time comes. That's why it's crucial to make sure your loved ones know how to track down key documents in the first place.

In the event that your estate plan can't be found, your assets will be considered intestate—as if you didn't have a will—and will be divvied up according to state law. That, of course, totally defeats the purpose of the time and money that you spent carefully crafting your wishes in advance.

In most cases, your lawyer or other estate advisers, such as an insurance agent, will keep copies of your estate plan—but make sure that your designated executors, agents or trustees know who your advisers are. If not, survivors will end up searching through your house and files and contacting other friends and relatives for clues to your affairs.

To prevent a futile paper chase, let your loved ones know where your documents are stored, especially if they are serving as agents, executors, guardians or trustees. Some documents, such as organ donation forms, need to be accessed immediately, or they are useless. Some people even leave detailed letters of instruction for loved ones, providing names of and contact information for key advisers, financial accounts and insurance policies. *The Beneficiary Book* (available at www.active-insights.com) allows you to compile your key records and documents in an easy-to-access format for your heirs.

Keep your estate-planning documents—your will, trusts, insurance policies, advance health care directives, power-of-attorney documents and burial plans—in secure, fireproof safes in your attorney's office, as well as in your home or, depending on state law, in a bank safe-deposit box. At home, try to use a fireproof safe, rather than storing your documents on your bookshelf or in a pile of papers on your desk.

What about bank safe-deposit boxes? Rules about accessing safe-deposit boxes vary by state, so ask your lawyer if he or she recommends keeping your documents in one. Under some state laws, safe-deposit boxes are sealed during probate, making it very difficult for loved ones to get quick access to documents stored there. Some banks, meanwhile, allow survivors with proper documentation to search a decedent's safe-deposit box for a will, as long as they're accompanied by a bank employee (to prevent pilfering). If the key is missing, banks often can drill open the box, but usually for a fee of several hundred dollars.

You can also keep digital copies of your documents in password-protected online repositories, such as www.assetlock.net or www.legacylocker.com. (If you use such digital storage services, though, make sure to tell your executors and beneficiaries how to access them when the time comes.) These services can also store other key digital data, such as passwords for financial accounts, email accounts or social networking sites.

In recent years, there has been a proliferation of electronic identification information, such as passwords, user IDs and answers to the "secure questions" that many financial services use for protection. Such information is especially important for automated payments that you may have set up during your lifetime. Survivors may not be able to halt

## PREVENTING THE PAPER CHASE

Here are some of the key documents and financial data that you'll want to keep accessible for your heirs or for your agent, in case you become incapacitated. Make sure to keep these in a secure location, such as a fireproof file cabinet or home safe. This is a good reminder to keep your documents and file cabinet organized and up to date!

- Documents related to your estate plan, including your will, trusts and powers of attorney.

- Financial accounts and investments (retirement accounts, savings accounts, certificates of deposit, stocks and bonds) along with contact information for the institutions that hold the accounts. If you have minor children, make sure to include any custodial or savings accounts you have for them.

- Insurance policies.

- Beneficiary designation forms for your retirement accounts.

- Bills that you regularly pay, such as utilities, cable and telephone.

- Mortgage or other debt documents.

- Credit card accounts.

- Title, registration and insurance for your car.

- Tax returns.

- Cemetery or funeral home information.

- Electronic identification information, such as passwords, user IDs and answers to the "secure questions" that many financial services use for protection.

online payments, such as cable bills or insurance premiums, or e-commerce transactions, such as an eBay sale, if they don't know passwords and user IDs. Executors are usually able to obtain passwords and IDs if they present a death certificate or other information required by the website or institution. But this can take time, so it's much easier if records of these things have been kept and made accessible. Keep the information on a flash drive or CD, and print out an extra copy, too.

It also helps heirs tremendously if your financial and personal files are organized, so they can track down bank and investment accounts and other assets. Of course, that's much easier said than done for most people. Recent tax returns are usually a great help to heirs, because they usually include names of financial institutions that paid interest or dividends—a clue to where your holdings are.

Also, if you hold many different savings and investment accounts, consider consolidating some of them, which can simplify matters for you and your heirs.

## UPDATING YOUR DOCUMENTS

Maybe you haven't looked at your will in years. It was made by a lawyer who lives in another state, back when you lived there decades ago.

Time to dust it off and make some changes to reflect your current circumstances. Chances are things have changed in your life—or in the tax laws—since you last made your plan.

There's another reason to revisit your will: all the consolidation in the banking industry. If you named a bank as the executor of your estate and your bank has been bought or sold recently, you may now have a new executor. Make sure you know who that person or institution is—and that you trust its judgment. Also, check that the fees to carry out your will haven't changed.

You don't have to adjust your estate plans every year. But it's smart to take a fresh look at your will anytime there's a significant change in your family, from a marriage or a divorce to the birth of kids or grandkids—even the purchase or sale of a house. A simple update to a will usually costs a couple of hundred dollars and involves a call and meeting with your estate lawyer.

You also need to remember to update beneficiary designations on retirement and financial accounts and insurance policies to reflect your current circumstances, such as a divorce, marriage or a birth of a child.

Here are some events that may trigger an update to your estate plans:

- Marriage or remarriage

- Divorce

- Death of a close loved one, such as a spouse or child

- Birth or adoption of a child

- Birth or adoption of a grandchild

- Your children are no longer minors

- Serious illness or loss of capacity for you or a close family member

- Major family rift

- Move to a different state

- Dramatic increase or decrease in your level of wealth or income

- Intend to take distributions from a retirement account soon

- Purchase or sale of real estate

- Purchase or sale of a family business

- Large charitable gift

- Death or incapacity of your chosen executor, trustee, guardian or agent

- Merger or acquisition of a bank or trust company that you chose to serve as a trustee or executor

- Major change in federal or state tax laws, such as an increase in the estate-tax exemption or a ban on a widely used tax shelter

Even if your life has been pretty static, you should take stock of your estate plan every three to five years. Chances are you may be unaware of new laws or new estate-planning tactics that could affect your wishes. A checkup will also ensure that you have backup guardians, executors and agents in place, in case the ones you chose have become unable to carry out your wishes.

In addition to updating your will or trust, make sure to update your power-of-attorney documents and health care directives. For instance, if you move to another state, your old documents may not be honored in your new state.

What's more, some estate-planning tools require regular follow-up, such as retitling assets, after you've established them. For instance, you may have set up a revocable living trust, but the vehicle is essentially useless if you don't get around to transferring your assets into the trust. Or a trust was supposed to be funded by life insurance that you never got around to buying. The bottom line: follow through on any documents that you have drafted.

## PARTING THOUGHTS

Alas, there's no magic bullet to evade death or taxes. But planning your financial and legal affairs ahead of time, while you're still in good health and of sound mind, can help reduce the pain of both events for your family. An estate plan is a lifelong process, one that changes and grows as you and your family evolve. And no matter how young you are, when it comes to planning ahead for your estate, it's never too early to start.

Regardless of what kind of estate plan you decide upon, the most important thing, by far, is to engage in open communication with your family members—to sit down with your loved ones and begin the process of talking about your plans and wishes for your family and possessions after you are gone. I hope that the *Wall Street Journal Complete Estate-Planning Guidebook* helps you get started on this very important endeavor.

# INDEX

# ABOUT THE AUTHOR

RACHEL EMMA SILVERMAN is an editor and reporter at the *Wall Street Journal,* where she has worked since 1998. She currently edits and cowrites The Juggle, the *Wall Street Journal's* work-and-family website, and reports on career, workplace and family issues. Before that, she covered personal finance, focusing on estate planning, wealth management, insurance, philanthropy, art and collectibles and financial aspects of marriage and divorce. She lives in Austin, Texas, with her husband and two young sons.

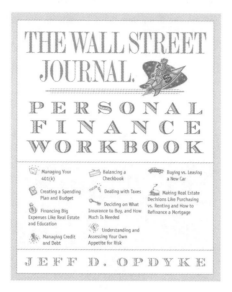

This hands-on, interactive guide to managing your personal finances makes it quick and easy to get your financial life in order and ultimately build wealth.

*The Wall Street Journal.*
*Personal Finance Workbook*

978-0-307-33601-9
$13.95 paperback (Canada: $21.00)

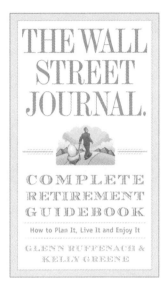

A blueprint for retirement planning,
this book will teach you how to tailor a
financial plan for a retirement that could
very well be the best part of your life.

*The Wall Street Journal.*
*Complete Retirement Guidebook*

978-0-307-35099-2
$14.95 paperback (Canada: $19.95)

Unravel the mysteries of financial markets in this
timely guide to investing in your future, from
college savings to retirement plans.

*The Wall Street Journal.*
*Complete Money & Investing Guidebook*

978-0-307-23699-9
$14.95 paperback (Canada: $21.00)

# The Wall Street Journal
## SPECIAL OFFER

## The One Investment You Can Count On.

# 2 WEEKS FREE!

YES! Send me 2 free weeks of *The Wall Street Journal* and also enter my subscription for an additional 26 weeks at the money-saving rate of only $59.00 – just 35¢ a day! I receive 28 weeks in all and SAVE OVER 50% off the regular rate.

Name

Address

City

State                              Zip

2PFALG

---

### CALL NOW FOR FASTER SERVICE!
# 1-866-509-3842

---

## THE WALL STREET JOURNAL.

The Guide in your hands is a great way to start building wealth.

The best way to keep your assets growing is to read THE WALL STREET JOURNAL!

Why Spending Too Much Time Online Could Make You a Nicer Person

**THE WALL STREET JOURNAL.**

Google's $12.5 Billion Gamble

Send in the card below and receive

# 2 WEEKS FREE!